# COUNTRY WALKS
# NEAR
# PHILADELPHIA

# COUNTRY WALKS
# NEAR
# PHILADELPHIA

by
## ALAN FISHER

Published by
## THE APPALACHIAN MOUNTAIN CLUB
BOSTON, MASSACHUSETTS
1983

COUNTRY WALKS NEAR PHILADELPHIA

FIRST EDITION          5   4   3   2      87   88   89

---

*Editorial supervision by Sally Greene Carrel*
*Cover Design by Janis Capone*
*Photos and maps by Alan Fisher*
*Composition by Pamela Boord, Cheryl Dunphy, and Claudia Majetich*
*Production by Michael Cirone and Nancy H. Maynes*

---

ISBN 0-910146-42-X

# CONTENTS

*ness. Starting at the mouth of the valley, where
Wissahickon Creek joins the Schuylkill River, a
bicycle path and a former carriage road follow the
creek upstream to Valley Green Inn. Return on a
bridle path along the east slope of the valley.*

*Walking and ski touring — 4 miles (6.4 kilometers).
From Bells Mill Road to Valley Green on a winding
carriage road that is closed to motor vehicles. The
route follows the bottom of the gorge next to Wissahickon Creek. Return on a bridle path along the
side of the valley.*

*Walking — 1 or more miles (1.6 or more kilo-
meters). A private nature preserve of five hundred
acres. Six miles of foot trails lead through meadows,
weedy fields, and wooded ravines where the Upper
Roxborough highlands slope toward the Schuylkill
River.*

*Walking — 1 or more miles (1.6 or more kilo-
meters). A magnificent country estate planted with
thousands of varieties of native and exotic trees and
shrubs. The Morris mansion is gone, but the lawns,
ponds, formal gardens, and other landscape features remain.*

*Walking and ski touring — 8 miles (12.9 kilo-
meters). A linear park cutting across northeastern
Philadelphia. Drop out of the city into a quiet,
wooded valley. Follow bicycle paths and horse trails
next to Pennypack Creek.*

## 9 Pennypack Creek
## Northern Section

*Walking and ski touring — 6 miles (9.7 kilometers). Easy trails through a narrow, wooded valley. A bicycle path stretches along Pennypack Creek between the bridges at Roosevelt Boulevard and Pine Road. Return on a bridle path along the eastern bank.*

## 10 Tyler State Park

*Walking and ski touring — 7.5 miles (12.1 kilometers). A network of bicycle paths, horse trails, and tree-lined country roads closed to motor vehicles. The route follows Neshaminy Creek upstream to the Schofield Ford covered bridge. Return through rolling farmland and woods.*

## 11 Rancocas State Park

*Walking and ski touring — 3 miles (4.8 kilometers). Dirt roads and footpaths lead through a flat landscape of woods and weedy fields. At times the trail overlooks Rancocas Creek.*

## 12 Delaware Canal
## Yardley south to Morrisville
## Yardley north to Washington Crossing

*Walking and ski touring — up to 17 miles (27.4 kilometers) roundtrip. From Yardley south or north on the broad, level towpath of the Delaware Canal. Four miles south of Yardley is Morrisville. Four miles north of Yardley is the McConkey's Ferry section of Washington Crossing Historic Park, where the Continental Army crossed the Delaware River to attack Trenton. Four and a half miles farther north along the canal is the Thompson's Mill section of the Washington Crossing Historic Park. Hike as far as you want and return by the way you came.*

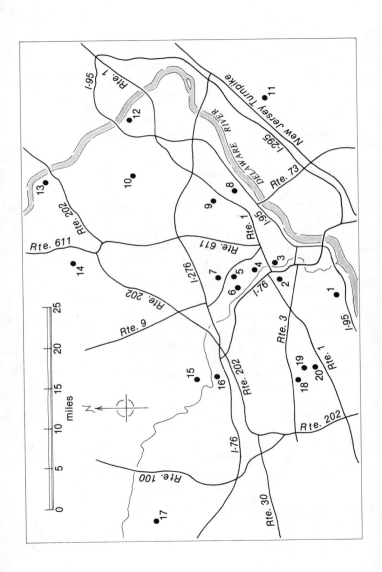

# PREFACE

THERE'S STILL TIME for a walk in the woods, even if you've spent all morning working or sleeping late.

This book is for people who want an outing in the country without wasting half the day getting there and coming back. If you live in the Philadelphia region, the excursions described here are close at hand. All but one (Hopewell Village) are within reach of the city by public transportation; all are easily reached by car. The walks have been planned to show the best parts of Philadelphia's countryside and to encourage everyone to use the many large parks and extensive trail networks maintained by federal, state, county, and city agencies and private conservation groups.

Each chapter of this book includes directions, a map, and a commentary on the area's natural or social history. The routes cover the gamut of southeastern Pennsylvania's Piedmont and Coastal Plain landscapes: steep-sided river valleys, rolling hills, flood plains, woods, farmland, meadow, and marsh, as well as historic houses, mill sites, and ruins along the way. All the areas included here are open to the public, and many are excellent for ski touring as well as for walking. The excursions are attractive at all times of year, and successive visits during different seasons — to see the changing foliage, views, flowers, birds, and wildlife — provide an added dimension of enjoyment.

Although the routes described here are not rugged, a few precautions are in order. Wear shoes that you do not mind getting muddy or wet. Sneakers or thick-soled running shoes are adequate (except in cold weather); hiking shoes or boots are better. I usually carry a small knapsack containing a few sandwiches, a plastic waterbottle, a sweater, a rain parka, and some insect repellent in summer and early fall. During the warmer months check your clothing and body for ticks when you return from your walk. In the relatively few instances where the routes follow roads for short distances, walk on the left shoulder facing the oncoming traffic. To help maintain the trails free from drooping branches, you may want to bring a small pair of shears. And remember when allotting time that two miles per hour is a typical walking pace for a leisurely excursion.

If you plan to take a bus or train of the Southeastern Pennsylvania Transportation Authority (SEPTA), always call 574-7800 beforehand to check on the route, schedule, and connections for the trip both out and back. Telephone numbers for other transportation companies are included in the text. Specify the day you are thinking of going; schedules and routes frequently are different for weekdays, Saturday, Sunday, and holidays.

The following people helped me by providing information or other assistance for this book: Yolanda Alcorta of the John J. Tyler Arboretum; Gerald E. Franz of the Tinicum National Environmental Center; Patty Hurter; Dick James of the Schuylkill Valley Nature Center for Environmental Education, Inc.; John Francis Marion of the Friends of Laurel Hill Cemetery; John McIlhenny, Fairmount Park Historian; Lois Minderjahn of the Philadelphia Conservationists, Inc.; and Dr. Gary Smith and Mrs. Karen Smith. Very many thanks.

A.F.

# 1

# TINICUM NATIONAL ENVIRONMENTAL CENTER

*Walking and ski touring — 3 miles (4.8 kilometers). The path follows a dike between a freshwater lagoon and a broad tidal marsh at the mouth of Darby Creek. Return on a wide trail through scrub and woods. Good birding. Open daily from 8:00 A.M. until sunset. Dogs must be leashed. Picnicking is prohibited. Managed by the U.S. Fish and Wildlife Service (visitor center: 365-3118; headquarters: 521-0662).*

---

ABOUT 325 SPECIES OF BIRDS are seen regularly in the Delaware Valley and southern New Jersey. Looking for them can take you as far afield as the Pocono Mountains, Hawk Mountain, the New Jersey coast, and Bombay Hook bordering Delaware Bay. Or you can drive (or ride the bus) 6 miles from downtown Philadelphia to Tinicum National Environmental Center in the southwestern corner of the city. Over 280 species — about 85 percent of the Delaware Valley and New Jersey bird lists — have been recorded at Tinicum's shallow lake, fields, thickets, woods, mud flats, and freshwater tidal marsh.

In late winter and early spring huge numbers of geese, ducks, grebes, and coots pass through the refuge on their way north. They are followed by herons, egrets, ibises, myriad shore birds, and the usual land birds of eastern Pennsylvania and New Jersey. Over 75 species nest at Tinicum, including harriers, kestrels, quail, herons, bitterns, rails, owls, and many songbirds and waterfowl. In late summer the shore birds return to feed on the mud flats. Migrating hawks and owls also pause at

the refuge. By fall waterfowl crowd the impoundment and creek. Some stay for the winter, as do many ducks if the lake and creek do not freeze. Call or stop by the visitor center to learn what unusual birds have been spotted recently, and look for them as you walk.

The concentration of birds at Tinicum is all the more remarkable for occurring within sight of downtown Philadelphia, in a sector of the city that for the most part has been given over to tank farms, factories, and new housing developments. About 90 percent of the tidal marshland that formerly bordered the Delaware River between Darby Creek and the Schuylkill River has been filled in during the last half-century, yet Tinicum continues to be a major stopover on the Atlantic flyway. Delaware Bay funnels northbound waterfowl and shore birds through the Philadelphia region. Land birds are deflected along the bay's western shore and up the Delaware Valley. Heading south, many birds again follow the Delaware River. For some species, nearly 150 acres of wild rice at Tinicum provide food.

In geologic terms, Tinicum's low marsh landscape is of extremely recent origin. When the continental glacier that covered Canada, the Great Lakes region, New England, New York, and northeastern Pennsylvania began its final retreat about ten thousand or twelve thousand years ago, an immense quantity of water was released and the level of the sea rose. The ocean flooded the lower Delaware Valley to create Delaware Bay. Then, as now, rivers carrying mud in suspension dumped their load of sediment as their currents dissipated in the estuary. In this manner the Tinicum region became an extensive settling basin. Test borings at Tinicum show deposits of sand, silt, and clay as thick as 28 feet.

Although Darby Creek is tidal to the 84th Street bridge and the Delaware River is tidal as far north as Trenton, the downstream current usually prevents salt water from reaching Tinicum Marsh. Wild rice, which is extremely sensitive to saline conditions, flourishes in the upper tidal zone. However, the relative sparsity of rice in the lower mud flats near the mouth of the creek suggests that brackish water, which is heavier than fresh water,

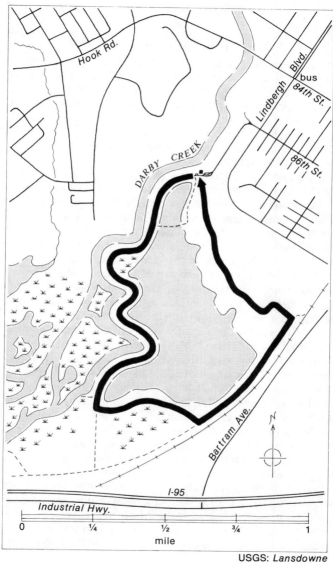

Hook Rd.

DARBY CREEK

Lindbergh Blvd.

bus

84th St.

86th St.

Bartram Ave.

N

I-95

Industrial Hwy.

| 0 | ¼ | ½ | ¾ | 1 |

mile

occasionally creeps upstream in the bottom of the channels during periods of low flow.

Because of the constant influx of nutrient-laden mud and the unfailing flow of water, whether salt or fresh, tidal marshes achieve extraordinary natural productivity. Their warm, sunlit waters enable photosynthesis to take place at a rapid rate. Great quantities of algae and animal microorganisms are produced; algae are even able to grow during the winter. Insects, worms, snails, mollusks, crustaceans, and bait fish thrive on the algae and rotting vegetation. Although stream pollution has left Tinicum with only a meager variety of invertebrates and fish compared to less-contaminated wetlands, its marsh still yields more vegetable matter than the most fertile farmland. Studies at Tinicum indicate that the stands of wild rice, so important to waterfowl, produce yearly about 7 tons per acre of organic matter (including stems and leaves) compared to 1½ tons for wheat fields and 4½ tons for the very best hay land.

The fertility of the alluvial soil at Tinicum, and the ease of enclosing large treeless tracts of marsh with dikes and converting the meadows to conventional agriculture, were not lost on the European settlers. Tinicum Island — located at the mouth of Darby Creek, and the site of one of the first European communities in the Delaware Valley — was settled by Swedes under Johann Printz in 1643, five years after an earlier Swedish settlement at Christiana (now Wilmington) and forty years before William Penn founded Philadelphia. At the time of the Swedish settlement, Tinicum Island, which now is merged physically with the surrounding land, was an isolated hill overlooking a broad marshy plain that was flooded at high tide. Printz established his colony here because it was near Dutch Fort Nassau at present-day Gloucester, New Jersey. Printz thought that the new base of Swedish activity at Tinicum would enjoy an advantage in trade with the Indians to the west and would thwart the expansion of the New Netherlands colony centered at New Amsterdam on Manhattan Island. In 1655, however, the Swedish colony was annexed by New Netherlands. The Dutch in turn gave way to the English, who in 1664 seized New Amsterdam and all the Dutch outposts south to Delaware.

A system of dikes enclosing the vast stretches of tidal marsh along the Delaware River between Darby Creek and the Schuyl-kill River was well established by the time of the Revolutionary War. Planted in hay, the diked flats were used to graze cattle and sheep. By 1788 the Pennsylvania legislature had passed four acts governing the maintenance and extension of the dikes. A map dating from the middle of the nineteenth century bears a note superimposed over the area now occupied by Philadelphia International Airport: "Flats formerly covered by reeds and bushes and partially submerged at high water, now reclaimed from the tides by banks."

Management of the system of dikes and drainage courses was the responsibility of two companies comprising owners of the enclosed land. According to a 1936 report of the U.S. Army Corps of Engineers, the companies eventually were dissolved during the first decade of the twentieth century. Earlier, the dikes had deteriorated and for a period of time the enclosed land had reverted to marshy meadows.

However, development of efficient hydraulic dredges during the late nineteenth century portended the obliteration of most of the wetlands. These machines suck mud from the bottom of a river or harbor and pump the material through a floating line to areas to be filled on shore. It was only a matter of time before the technique was applied to the Delaware River and its bordering wetlands. At the outset of World War I, 400 acres of marsh at Hog Island east of Tinicum were filled for a shipyard. During the 1930s the site of Philadelphia International Airport was filled hydraulically with an estimated hundred million cubic feet of sand and silt pumped from the Delaware ship channel. Other large sections of marsh, including tracts now within the bound-aries of the refuge, were buried at intervals. The last such operation occurred in the early 1970s.

Efforts to preserve at least some of Tinicum Marsh began in 1952, when a committee of the Delaware Valley Ornithological Club proposed to Mayor Joseph A. Clark, Jr., that Philadelphia establish a municipal wildlife refuge. The mayor's response was encouraging, but as the committee explored the matter it learned that Gulf Oil Corporation, owner of the land, had already contracted with the Corps of Engineers and state and local agencies to let the area be used as a basin for spoil dredged from the Schuylkill River. Eventually another site was found for disposal of the silt. In 1953 Philadelphia Conservationists, Inc., was organized to continue working for the creation of a wildlife preserve. After assurance that its pipeline rights-of-way would be protected, Gulf Oil agreed to donate the land to Philadelphia, and in 1955 the city established the Tinicum Wildlife Refuge. Comprising at first only 145 acres, the preserve included the dike, lake, and woods at the eastern end of the present-day refuge.

The remaining wetlands at Tinicum were threatened in the late 1960s by highway plans to route I-95 through the area. Part of the expressway was in fact built through the western stretches of Tinicum Marsh before national and local conservation groups and area congressmen convinced the federal Department of the Interior that the area should be added to the National Wildlife Refuge System. In 1971 the unfinished portion of the highway was realigned along the southern edge of the marsh, and the following year Congress created the Tinicum National Environmental Center.

The refuge at Tinicum now totals about 900 acres, including the city's original preserve, which was transferred to the U.S. Fish and Wildlife Service. Acquisition of an additional 300 acres is being negotiated. A master plan completed in 1979 proposes a long-range program to restore former tidal wetlands and to dig several freshwater ponds immediately southwest of the present impoundment. Other filled areas will be managed as forests or fields to create a wide diversity of wildlife habitats.

*PUBLIC TRANSIT:    From Snyder station near the southern end of the Broad Street subway line, take SEPTA bus 37 toward International Airport via Passyunk Avenue, 61st Street, and Lindbergh Boulevard. Get off at the intersection*

*of Lindbergh Boulevard and 84th Street. You will know that
your stop is coming after the bus passes Island Avenue and
80th Street.*

*From the bus stop walk south on Lindbergh Boulevard ¼
mile to the entrance of Tinicum National Environmental
Center on the right. Follow the entrance road several hundred
yards to the visitor center.*

*AUTOMOBILE: The entrance to Tinicum National En-
vironmental Center is located on Lindbergh Boulevard a
short distance south of the intersection with 84th Street.
There are several approaches.*

*From downtown go south on Broad Street to the intersec-
tion with Pattison Avenue, which crosses Broad Street just
south of Veterans Stadium and north of the Spectrum. Turn
right onto Pattison Avenue. Alternatively, from I-76 (just
west of the Walt Whitman Bridge), exit for Broad Street.
Follow Broad Street south for 0.4 mile, then turn right onto
Pattison Avenue. As a third possibility, from I-95 turn north
onto Broad Street and then, after 0.4 mile, turn left onto
Pattison Avenue. In any of these cases, follow Pattison
Avenue west 0.9 mile to an intersection with Penrose Ave-
nue. Turn left onto Penrose Avenue and cross high above the
Schuylkill River. At Airport Circle 1.2 miles west of the river,
turn right onto Island Avenue. Follow Island Avenue 0.4 mile
to an intersection with Bartram Avenue. Turn left onto
Bartram Avenue and go 0.3 mile to an intersection with 84th
Street. Turn right onto 84th Street and continue 0.7 mile to
an intersection with Lindbergh Boulevard. Turn left onto
Lindbergh Boulevard and go 0.2 mile to the entrance to
Tinicum National Environmental Center on the right. Follow
the entrance drive several hundred yards to the parking lot
and visitor center.*

*Another approach starts on I-95 about two miles east of
Chester. Exit from I-95 onto Route 420 south to Essington.
After a short distance turn left (east) onto Route 291. Follow
Route 291 for 2.2 miles, then turn left onto Bartram Avenue.*

Follow Bartram Avenue north 1.5 miles to the intersection with 84th Street. Turn left onto 84th Street and continue 0.7 mile to an intersection with Lindbergh Boulevard. Turn left onto Lindbergh Boulevard and go 0.2 mile to the entrance to Tinicum National Environmental Center on the right. Follow the entrance drive several hundred yards to the parking lot and visitor center.

THE WALK:    From the visitor center follow the main path through a small parking lot and out along the top of the broad dike, which the federal Work Projects Administration (WPA) and state and county governments reconstructed during the 1930s on the site of an earlier dike. On the left is a freshwater impoundment; on the right is tidal Darby Creek. Continue 1¼ miles on the winding dike road, at one point passing a boardwalk leading left across the impoundment. Check for birds from the observation tower.

   Where the road reaches a broad, weedy clearing, look for birds on the mud flats to the right (if the tide is low). Turn left to continue around the edge of the impoundment. Descend from the dike where the road veers sharply right about 100 yards from an expressway. Turn left and continue around the impoundment. Follow the dirt road all the way back to the parking lot and visitor center.

# 2

# FAIRMOUNT PARK

*Walking and ski touring — 3 miles (4.8 kilometers). A loop from Belmont Mansion to Chamounix and back on dirt roads and bridle paths. The route weaves through an extensive forest covering the western slope and tributary ravines of the Schuylkill Valley. Managed by the Fairmount Park Commission (686-2176 or 686-2177).*

---

**H**OW WOULD NEW YORK'S CENTRAL PARK appear if it were left to grow wild? What would happen to its Sheep Meadow, its curving drives, and its large masonry bridges separating vehicular and pedestrian traffic? An answer of sorts is provided by the overgrown fields of Philadelphia's old Ridgeland Farm, the disused carriage roads, and an abandoned stone bridge now nearly enveloped by forest in Fairmount Park west of the Schuylkill River and north of the Belmont Plateau. Here the walker can follow a system of little-used bridle paths through deep woods and new growth in a section of Fairmount unknown to most park visitors.

During the latter half of the eighteenth century, the land on both sides of the Schuylkill River north of "Faire Mount" (the rocky hill that is now the site of the Philadelphia Art Museum) comprised the private estates of some of Philadelphia's leading families. Prosperous merchants, bankers, shipowners, judges, and other members of the city's aristocracy of wealth established summer homes and farms along the highlands overlooking the river.

Some of these homes were at first simple farmhouses that later were improved and expanded; others were opulent man-

*Black-eyed Susan*, Rudbeckia hirta

sions from the start. Mount Pleasant, built atop the east bluff by sea captain and privateersman John Macpherson, was called by John Adams in 1775 "the most elegant seat in Pennsylvania." Between 1770 and 1799, financier Robert Morris had a farm and elaborate complex of gardens and greenhouses at The Hills just north of Faire Mount. After Morris's bankruptcy the property was acquired by Henry Pratt, who erected the Lemon Hill mansion. In 1797 Samuel Breck, later a state senator and congressman, built Sweetbriar on the west bank to escape the yellow-fever epidemic that killed ten thousand Philadelphians in the older part of the city between 1793 and 1800. These and more than a dozen other eighteenth- and nineteenth-century houses still stand within the park. Many have been restored, handsomely furnished, and opened to the public. An easy way to tour these remarkable mansions is via the Fairmount trolley bus, which circles the park between 10:00 A.M. and 4:30 P.M., Wednesday through Sunday, April through October. A guided tour, arranged through the Park Houses Office of the Philadelphia Museum of Art, provides a more informative approach. Telephone 763-8100, extension 304, for more information.

Between 1812 and 1822 Philadelphia excavated a reservoir atop Faire Mount and constructed the Fairmount waterworks and dam to supply the city with drinking water. (The museum basement now occupies the reservoir.) In the following years pressure slowly mounted for public acquisition of the land bordering the river, in order to both protect the purity of the water and provide a park for the growing city. A small public garden at the waterworks was expanded in 1844 by the purchase of Pratt's Garden at Lemon Hill, a tract of 45 acres that previously had been open to the public on an admission-fee basis. In 1855 this land was dedicated as Fairmount Park. Sedgely, an estate of 34 acres to the north of Lemon Hill, was acquired by the city in 1857.

Galvanized into action by the realization that Philadelphia's "cup of water was in danger of becoming a poisoned chalice," the state legislature established the Fairmount Park Commission in 1867 and authorized the city to expand Fairmount "as open

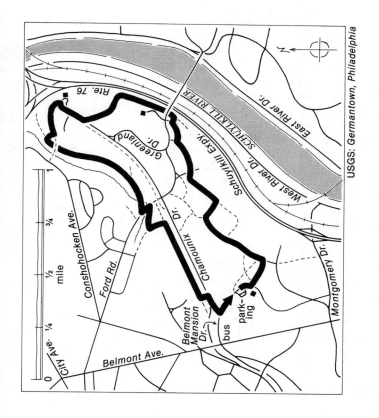

USGS: Germantown, Philadelphia

17

public ground and Park for the preservation of Schuylkill water and of the health and enjoyment of the people forever." Still larger appropriations of land, including the Wissahickon Valley, were approved in 1868. During the next few years the city purchased the estates of Mount Pleasant, Woodford, Solitude, Sweetbriar, Belmont, Ridgeland, Chamounix, and hundreds of other properties large and small. Jesse George and his sister donated the land at Georges Hill. Chemical works, breweries, paper and cotton mills, carpet and dye works, and other factories along the Schuylkill River and Wissahickon Creek were acquired and demolished.

By 1868 the park land along the Schuylkill and Wissahickon valleys totaled 4,077 acres. By comparison, New York's Central Park, established in 1854, totals 840 acres. Maps published in conjunction with the Centennial Exhibition, a world's fair held in western Fairmount in 1876 to celebrate the nation's first hundred years of independence, show a configuration of park boundaries and roads little different from what exists today. However, the northwest sector of the park — the area explored by this walk — was still largely undeveloped, and so it remains to this day.

*PUBLIC TRANSIT: SEPTA bus 38 passes near the start of the walk at Belmont Mansion in Fairmount Park.*

*Approaching from the north, catch bus 38 from Bala Cynwyd at the intersection of City Avenue and Conshohocken State Road. This intersection is ½ block east of Bala station on the Ivy Ridge—Manayunk railroad line from Penn Center and 30th Street stations. As the bus heads south on Belmont Avenue, get off at the intersection with Georges Hill Drive (which on the east side of Belmont Avenue becomes Belmont Mansion Drive). You will know that your stop is coming when the bus passes Conshohocken Avenue and then Edgeley Avenue on the right.*

*Approaching from the south, bus 38 travels from downtown Philadelphia to Fairmount Park via Chestnut Street, JFK Boulevard, and Girard Avenue. You will know that your*

*stop is coming when the bus turns north onto Belmont Avenue
and then passes Montgomery Drive on the right.*

*From the bus stop at the intersection of Belmont Avenue
and Belmont Mansion Drive, walk east ¼ mile to a parking
lot on the right.*

*AUTOMOBILE:    From the intersection of City Avenue
(Route 1) and Belmont Avenue 1 mile west of the Schuylkill
River, follow Belmont Avenue south 0.7 mile. Turn left onto
Belmont Mansion Drive and go 0.2 mile to a parking lot on
the right serving Belmont Mansion and Playhouse in the
Park.*

*Alternatively, from the intersection of Belmont and Girard
avenues 1 mile west of the Schuylkill River, follow Belmont
Avenue north 1 mile. Turn right onto Belmont Mansion Drive
and go 0.2 mile to the parking lot on the right.*

*THE WALK:    From the parking lot north of Belmont Man-
sion, cross Belmont Mansion Drive. Follow the road right
several hundred yards downhill to a point where a broad
view stretches left over the park and downtown Philadelphia.*

The oldest part of Belmont Mansion predates 1742, when the
property was purchased by Judge William Peters. His estate of
more than 200 acres extended from the Schuylkill River to a point
approximately 2,000 feet west of present-day Belmont Avenue.
In 1755 the house was greatly enlarged by the addition of the first
two floors of the section that now overlooks the city to the
southeast.

William Peters was a loyalist who returned to England during
the Revolution, but his son Richard was a patriot who served as
secretary of the Continental Board of War and later as a member
of the Continental Congress and a judge of the U.S. District Court
of Pennsylvania for thirty-seven years. Described by his neighbor
Samuel Breck of Sweetbriar as "unceremonious, communica-
tive, friendly," Richard Peters developed Belmont into a model
farm and country seat where George Washington, James Madi-

son, Benjamin Franklin, and other national leaders dined during the period from 1790 to 1800, when Philadelphia was the capital of the new republic. Breck wrote of Peters:

> The playfulness of his conversation always enlivened by flashes of the gayest pleasantry was forever quick and unrestrained and varied by casts of true humour, sometimes as broad and well enacted as the most exaggerated farce, and at others convolved in double meaning, fit only for the ready perception of the most practiced ear and polished taste . . . .
> When a morning of leisure permitted that great man [Washington] to drive to Belmont . . . .it was his constant habit to do so. There, sequestered from the world, and the torments and cares of his business, Washington would enjoy . . .a wholly unceremonious intercourse with the judge, walking for hours side by side, in the beautiful gardens of Belmont, beneath the dark shade of lofty hemlocks placed there by his ancestors a century ago.

During the Centennial Exhibition of 1876, Belmont Mansion and its garden were a European-style cafe. In recent years the mansion has sometimes functioned as a restaurant open in the summer during the season of Playhouse in the Park, which is adjacent.

*Turn half-left off the road in front of Belmont Mansion and follow the edge of the woods downhill. Head slightly to the left of the distant dome of Memorial Hall, which served as the art gallery for the Centennial Exhibition and is now the headquarters for the Fairmount Park Commission and park police. Near the bottom of the hill turn left onto an asphalt drive that leads to a maintenance area enclosed by a chain link fence. Turn left again onto a gravel road in front of the chain link enclosure. Follow the gravel road into the woods.*

This road almost immediately passes the old inclined plane (sloping uphill to the left) of the Philadelphia and Columbia

Railroad — later the Pennsylvania Railroad. Trains were hauled up the hill or let down by a cable and steam winch.

The gravel road continues through a forest that was once part of Ridgeland Farm, which during the first half of the nineteenth century was the summer home of Jacob S. Waln, a member of the City Council and Pennsylvania legislature. The Federal-style, three-story Ridgeland house, built in 1719, is uphill to the left out of sight of the path. The house now is occupied by a member of the Fairmount Park staff.

*Continue through the woods. Eventually fork right where the other fork climbs left uphill. Continue through an area that is half clearing and half scrub. Re-enter the woods and turn left at a T-intersection. Follow the path straight through the woods, then to the right. Cross the entrance drive to a recycling center. Continue downhill and across a small bridge. Turn right to continue through the woods. Just before the trail reaches Greenland Drive, fork right downhill, then turn left where the old roadbed of the Fairmount trolley passes under Greenland Drive.*

The Fairmount trolley system was built during 1896—1897 and operated until 1946. One terminus was at the intersection of Belmont Avenue and Elm (now Parkside) near the former exhibition grounds. The other terminus was at 33rd and Dauphin streets. The trolley crossed the Schuylkill River on the Strawberry Mansion bridge. One arm of the system followed the flank of the valley north around Chamounix and south along the western edge of the park.

Greenland house, located a few dozen yards toward the river from the former trolley underpass, recalls the name of Greenland Village, an intended land development that never came to fruition. The house is occupied by a member of the park staff.

*With the Schuylkill Expressway on the right, continue straight past two paths intersecting from the left, the second*

*of which leads to Lilacs, a plastered stone farmhouse later
enlarged by Philadelphia gentry and now occupied by park
personnel. Curve left uphill to a field. Cross the field diagonally toward the stable of the mounted park police. Follow
Chamounix Drive right. At the end of the road (with
Chamounix Mansion within sight to the right) continue
straight on a driveway just to the right of a smaller building
(the Chamounix carriage house).*

Yet another nineteenth-century country seat, Chamounix
Mansion was built in 1800 by George Plumstead, a Quaker
merchant whose father and grandfather had been mayors of
Philadelphia. In 1806 the property was purchased by Benjamin
Johnson (the would-be developer of Greenland Village), who
moved here with his family from Ridgeland Farm, which he
sold to Jacob Waln. After the park acquired Chamounix from
the Johnsons in 1867, the house became a restaurant.

Chamounix is now the Philadelphia headquarters for the
American Youth Hostels Association. It has dormitory accom-
modations and cooking facilities for more than sixty visitors.
Telephone 878-3676 for information.

*From the carriage house at the entrance of the Chamounix
driveway, follow the looping driveway counter-clockwise for
90 yards. Turn abruptly left on a very faint footpath leading
downhill across the grass and into the woods. The trail,
which becomes much clearer as soon as it enters the woods,
is a former carriage road that used to link Falls Road (now
Conshohocken Avenue) with Chamounix. Follow the path
downhill to the left. Continue to a low stone parapet (actually
part of a bridge that has been overgrown by brush). Descend
very steeply to the right of the parapet, then turn left and
follow the path under the bridge. Again, this path is the
former roadbed of the Fairmount trolley.*

*With an apartment tower and a small stream on the right,
continue more or less straight, at one point passing a trail
intersecting from the left. At Ford Road turn left over the*

*stream, then right into a weedy meadow on the south side of the road. (On the left notice the stone abutments of a former trolley bridge over Ford Road.)*

*After crossing Ford Road, continue half-right through the meadow toward another apartment building. There is no trail. At the end of the building, turn left onto a decrepit asphalt road (which once served a trolley station.) Turn right at the end of the road. Follow a footpath into the woods and along the old roadbed. (A short walk in the opposite direction leads to a crumbling station platform on the left.)*

*Continue on the old trolley roadbed. At a picnic area turn left off the path. Cross a parking lot, and then cross Chamounix Drive. Turn right along the road, with an old iron railing on the left. (At a gap in the railing, notice a flight of stone stairs leading downhill into a thicket.) At a fork in the road, continue straight across a stone bridge to Belmont Mansion Drive. Turn left to return to the parking lot next to Belmont Mansion.*

# 3

# LAUREL HILL CEMETERY

*Walking — 1 or more miles (1.6 or more kilometers). A nineteenth-century garden cemetery. A forest of elaborate monuments and mausoleums stretches along the crest of the high bluff bordering the Schuylkill River near Strawberry Mansion bridge. Open 9:00 A.M. to 5:00 P.M. every day except Sunday. (Call the cemetery on weekdays to check for accessibility on the following Sunday.) Dogs must be leashed. Picnicking is prohibited. Managed by the Laurel Hill Cemetery Company (228-8200).*

---

LAUREL HILL was Philadelphia's first garden cemetery. During the nineteenth century it was not only a burial ground for the city's more prosperous families but also a favorite destination for rural excursions. Steamboats carried sightseers up and down the Schuylkill River between the waterworks dam and Manayunk, stopping at various landings and restaurants along the way. These excursions became so popular that the newly organized Fairmount Park Commission authorized the construction of landings at Fountain Green, Edgely Point, Strawberry Mansion, and Falls of Schuylkill on the east bank, and at Landsdowne Island, Belmont, and Ford Road on the west bank. The commission collected one penny for each person carried by the steamboats. An outing could include riverside refreshments (perhaps strawberries and cream at Strawberry Mansion) and a stroll through the nearby cemetery at Laurel Hill.

With its elaborate tombs and dramatic setting above the river, Laurel Hill appealed to the eclectic nineteenth-century taste for picturesque scenery, exotic artifacts, and sentimental refinement. The age romanticized death. Nathaniel Parker Willis, a widely read journalist of the day, wrote:

[W]e made an excursion to Laurel Hill, certainly the most beautiful cemetery in the world, after the Necropolis of Scutari. It seems as if it were intended to associate the visits of the departed more with our pleasures than our duties . . . . The views down upon the river and through the sombre glades and alleys of the burial ground, are unsurpassed for sweetness and repose.

A nineteenth-century print depicting Laurel Hill shows men in frock coats and top hats, and women with ground-length dresses, bonnets, and parasols. Some pause to read the inscriptions on the monuments while others walk arm-in-arm among the myriad obelisks, broken columns, sculptured urns, sarcophagi, little temples, stone crosses, angels, lambs (usually for children), and other expressive funereal emblems of the period.

Many of these monuments were substantial artistic commissions, reflecting to some extent the changing architectural styles of the nineteenth century. John Notman, an architect who laid out the paths, roads, and terraces for the first section of the cemetery, also designed the gatehouse in the neoclassic style introduced by Thomas Jefferson and Benjamin Latrobe. At virtually the same time he designed for Joseph S. Lewis, a leader in the creation of the Fairmount waterworks, a tomb with Egyptian motifs, often used at that time for funereal structures. Ten years later Notman designed for Sarah Harrison a cloister-like monument in the newly popular Gothic style. Art Nouveau elements are evident in some tombs from the end of the century. Simple geometric forms are typical of more modern memorials.

Laurel Hill Cemetery was established in 1836, when Philadelphia and other American cities were outgrowing their graveyards. Throughout the Colonial period and early nineteenth century, the usual practice here, as in England, was to bury the urban dead in common burial grounds next to churches. Noxious odors were said to rise from these overcrowded churchyards, which reformers of the day claimed were a menace to public health. Burial in common graveyards was deplored for its unseemliness as well. Final resting places were not at all final:

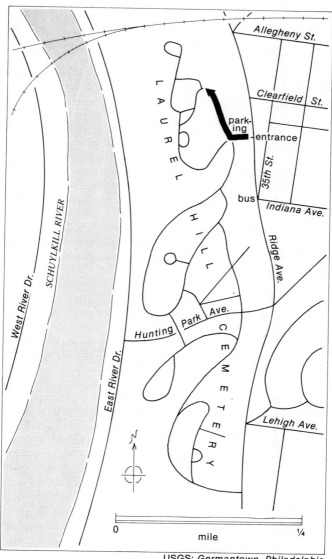

USGS: *Germantown, Philadelphia*

27

often bones were dug up to make way for the more recently dead. Also, the churchyards themselves were steadily diminished by urban encroachment.

Large, landscaped, rural cemeteries supported by the sale of private burial lots were proposed as an alternative to common burial grounds by Boston's Dr. Jacob Bigelow, a physician and botanist. He was a leading figure in the creation of Mount Auburn Cemetery in Cambridge, Massachusetts. Established in 1832 on a nonsectarian, commercial basis, Mount Auburn was the first garden cemetery in America, setting the pattern for what has since become the usual form of burial ground throughout the country.

Philadelphia followed in 1836 with the incorporation of Laurel Hill Cemetery. The cemetery company purchased Laurel, the country estate of Joseph Sims, and later bought the adjoining estates of Harleigh and Fairy Hill, at that time well beyond the limits of the city. Promotional literature declared that Laurel Hill was a place

> . . . where family affection could be gratified in the assurance that
> the remains of father and child, husband and wife could repose side
> by side undisturbed by the changing interests of man, where the
> smitten heart might pour out its grief over the grave of the cherished
> one, secure from the idle gaze of heartless passers-by, and where the
> mourner could rear a flower, consecrated to memory and hope.

From the outset Laurel Hill attracted the patronage of Philadelphia's leading families, many of whom moved the remains of their forebears to the new cemetery. Thus the tombs at Laurel Hill hold the bones of many eighteenth-century figures, including Andrew Bradford, publisher of the first newspaper in Pennsylvania and employer of Benjamin Franklin; David Rittenhouse, astronomer and clockmaker; General Jonathan Williams, chief of the army's Engineers Corps during the Revolutionary War; Thomas McKean, a signer of the Declaration of Independence; and Charles Thompson, secretary of the Continental Congress. In the course of the nineteenth century, numerous other distinguished citizens and thousands of people from among the city's merchant and professional families were buried at Laurel Hill.

The body of Colonel Ulric Dahlgren, a Union officer in the Civil War, arrived at Laurel Hill after an extraordinary odyssey. He was killed on March 2, 1864, during an unsuccessful attack on Richmond. After cutting off one of Dahlgren's fingers to obtain a ring and removing his wooden leg for use by their own veterans, the Confederates left his body in a field. Three days later the Confederate government released to the Richmond newspapers captured documents (the authenticity of which has long been disputed) revealing that Dahlgren had planned to burn Richmond and to kill Jefferson Davis and his cabinet if the city were taken. Union prisoners were compared to the Huns and Goths, and one publication urged that Dahlgren's body be exhibited as a "monument of infamy."

To prevent such a spectacle, Jefferson Davis ordered that the corpse be buried secretly without ceremony. The Richmond *Examiner* for March 8 stated, "It was a dog's burial, without coffin, winding sheet or service. [Actually, the corpse was buried in a rough box.] Friends and relatives at the North need inquire no further; this is all they will know — he is buried, a burial that befitted the mission upon which he came."

However, Dahlgren also had friends in the South. Elizabeth Van Lew, a Richmond lady who spied for the North, later wrote that "the heart of every loyal person was stirred to its depths by the outrage committed upon his inaminate body, and to discover the hidden grave and remove his honored dust to friendly care was decided upon." Miss Van Lew and her cohorts learned the location of Dahlgren's grave from a black worker and had the corpse, still identifiable by its missing leg and finger, removed clandestinely and reburied at yet another location on an outlying farm. Later, when Dahlgren's father requested the return of his son's body and Jefferson Davis consented, it was found to be missing from its supposed location. After the war, when Miss

Van Lew revealed the body's whereabouts, Dahlgren's remains were moved to Laurel Hill and placed in their third and final grave.

Time has taken its toll on Laurel Hill. Trust funds established at local banks by many lot holders more than a hundred years ago have proven insufficient for the upkeep of the monuments. Similarly, revenues from the cemetery's own funds and from the sale of the relatively few unused lots that remain have been inadequate to maintain the gatehouse, roads, and retaining walls. Air pollution and weathering have eroded some of the inscriptions. Nonetheless, Laurel Hill today has a timeworn charm and sense of pleasant desolation that is perhaps more fitting for a cemetery than the close-cropped and polished blandness of more modern burial grounds.

Moreover, in recent years Laurel Hill has again begun to attract the attention of sightseers. The cemetery has been listed on the National Register of Historic Places. The Friends of Laurel Hill Cemetery, a nonprofit corporation, conducts tours of the cemetery. Dues and other funds raised by the Friends are helping to restore the gatehouse and various sculpture groups and tombs. For further information about the activities of this organization, write to the Friends of Laurel Hill Cemetery, 3822 Ridge Avenue, Philadelphia, Pennsylvania 19132.

*PUBLIC TRANSIT: Laurel Hill Cemetery is passed by SEPTA bus 61 running on Ridge Avenue between the intersection of 9th and Sansom streets in downtown Philadelphia and Manayunk in northwest Philadelphia. Approaching from the south, you will know that your stop is coming when the bus passes between cemeteries on both sides of the road and then goes by Hunting Park Avenue. From the north, Allegheny Avenue and Clearfield Street on the left signal the approach of your stop. Get off the bus at the intersection of Ridge Avenue and 35th Street.*

*AUTOMOBILE: The entrance to Laurel Hill Cemetery is on the west side of Ridge Avenue 1 mile southeast of the interchange linking Ridge Avenue, City Avenue (Route 1), East River Drive, and Wissahickon Drive. Park inside the main cemetery gate.*

*THE WALK:    Fork right from the main gate and then stroll south through the cemetery along the slopes and terraces overlooking the Schuylkill River.*

**4**

# WISSAHICKON VALLEY
## Southern Section

*Walking and ski touring — 7.5 miles (12 kilometers).*
*Philadelphia's celebrated intown wilderness, described by*
*Baedeker as "an Alpine gorge in miniature."*
*Starting at the mouth of the valley, where Wissahickon Creek*
*joins the Schuylkill River, a bicycle path and a former carriage*
*road follow the creek upstream to Valley Green Inn. Return on a*
*bridle path along the east slope of the valley. Managed by the*
*Fairmount Park Commission (686-2176 or 686-2177).*

---

Ho! Away for the Wissahickon
For the dance and good stewed chicken.
Catfish! Waffles! Good hot toddy,
Cheers the heart and warms the body.
Swiftly gliding o'er the snow,
Merrily away we go.

THIS SLEIGHING SONG celebrates the Wissahickon Valley
of the mid-nineteenth century. Taverns and roadhouses bordering the Schuylkill River and Wissahickon Creek were popular
haunts of the day. There were the Punch Bowl, Robin Hood
Tavern, Belmont Cottage, Lions at Falls, and other hostelries
along the Schuylkill, and the Indian Rock Hotel, Valley Green
Inn, Lotus Inn, Wissahickon Hall, Maple Spring Hotel, and the
Log Cabin on the Wissahickon. This last establishment featured
the added attraction of two black bears chained to a stagecoach
in front of the tavern, as well as a menagerie of owls, foxes,

monkeys, and other small animals. Not to be outdone, the nearby Maple Spring Hotel had a bear that was trained to open and guzzle bottles of carbonated mineral water, and a museum of curiously carved roots and other such objects collected by the proprietor, Joseph "Whittler" Smith. Writing in 1913 in his book of memoirs, Cornelius Weygandt recalled that when he was a child "a black bear on a chain at this tavern often drew my vote for a walk down the creek, if Father let us choose which way we should walk."

Contemporary guidebooks, advertisements, and memoirs like those of Weygandt almost invariably mention catfish and waffles as a particular delicacy of the period. In 1929 Weygandt reported a fishmonger as recalling, "There wasn't a hotel or a tavern or a restaurant anywhere you'd drive or boat out of Philadelphia didn't hang out a sign, 'catfish and waffles,' come March, and keep it hung until long about the fourth of July." Weygandt himself reminisced:

"Catfish and waffles" began with fried catfish and a relish. A steak of beef followed, with fried potatoes, generally stewed chicken and the waffles. And after the chicken and the waffles, the coffee. . . .

At one of the Wissahickon roadhouses the proprietor went through the hocus pocus of netting catfish from a great tank full of fish, telling you that they were caught in the creek "only yesterday," and that he would kill and cook for you the fish you had just seen netted. He carried the fish into the kitchen, from which, I suppose he carried them back to the tank as soon as you were out of the way. There were, doubtless, catfish for all waiting fully fried by the time patrons were likely to drop in.

So famous did this hostelry make its "catfish and waffles" that they became the combination for wedding dinners and brought hundreds of brides and grooms here for that important function. I know of one couple, wedded in 1857, to whom the Wissahickon remained always a place of pure romance because of such a visit. It was not Niagara, to be sure, the Mecca of subsequent generations of lovers, but it was a place of wild beauty, after its quiet fashion.

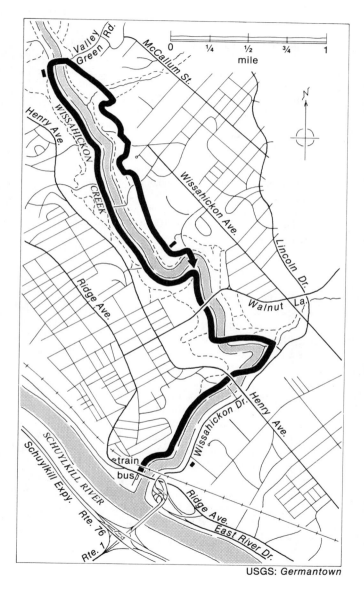

Valley Green Rd.

McCallum St.

N

0    ¼    ½    ¾    1
mile

Henry Ave.

WISSAHICKON CREEK

Wissahickon Ave.

Lincoln Dr.

Ridge Ave.

Walnut La.

Wissahickon Dr.

Henry Ave.

train
bus

SCHUYLKILL RIVER

Schuylkill Expy.    Rte. 76

Ridge Ave.

East River Dr.

Rte. 1

USGS: *Germantown*

35

And it could be visited again and its old memories renewed of a Sabbath, or of a holiday, even if one could not get a day's vacation when one yearned for it, as in this more hurried and less busy time.

Quantities of catfish formerly were caught in the Schuylkill River and in Wissahickon Creek. Charles V. Hagner, in his *Early History of the Falls of the Schuylkill,* wrote in 1869:

I have seen men, in one scoop of the dip-net, have it so full of these catfish as to be unable to lift them in the boat, but were obliged to take them out of it with their hands and other contrivances. . . . They came regularly on or about the 25th of May, the run of them lasting some two or three weeks. They were caught in immense numbers during the season, put in artificial ponds made for the purpose, and taken out as wanted during the summer and fall months. Thousands of people resorted to the hotels of the Falls to eat them. . . .

Weygandt recalled the mud "kicking with catfish" when the water was let out of the Germantown reservoir on Paper Mill Run, which flows into the Wissahickon. According to some accounts, the name Wissahickon itself is derived from the Delaware Indian term *Wisamikon,* supposedly meaning catfish stream, but others point to *Wissauchsickan,* meaning yellow-colored stream.

When the Wissahickon Valley was purchased by Philadelphia in 1868 for inclusion in Fairmount Park, the taverns — although allowed to remain open — languished and failed nonetheless. "But, alas," says Theo B. White in *Fairmount, Philadelphia's Park,* "with the acquisition of these inns and taverns, the commission imposed temperance. It is quite obvious that beer, wine, and whiskey were normal and desirable companions to a platter of catfish and waffles, and when such was denied, the patronage declined to extinction." Today only Valley Green Inn, midway up the Wissahickon Valley (and a destination of this walk), survives as an active restaurant. Wissahickon Hall, built near the lower end of the valley in 1849, is now a police station.

During the eighteenth century and continuing into the nineteenth, the Wissahickon Valley was also an important industrial center. Falling about 100 feet in a distance of 6½ miles, Wissahickon Creek provided water power for a series of grist-mills, sawmills, paper mills, textile mills, linseed oil mills, carpet and dye works, canneries, and other manufactories. The earliest was Robeson's Wissahickon Mill for producing flour, built at the mouth of the creek about 1686.

In 1683 Francis Daniel Pastorius emigrated from Germany and established Germantown just east of the lower Wissahickon Valley. Pastorius was the agent for the Frankfurt Land Company, a group of Frankfurt Quakers who bought the tract from William Penn. Also in 1683 the first permanent Mennonite settlement in America was made at Germantown.

Soon the German settlers began erecting mills along the upper stretches of Wissahickon Creek and its tributaries. William Rittenhouse, grandfather of the astronomer and clockmaker David Rittenhouse, was not only pastor of the new Mennonite community but also an early industrialist, who in 1690 established the first paper mill in the colonies. Remains of the mill and its surrounding village still stand on Paper Mill Run slightly above its confluence with Wissahickon Creek. Another German hamlet was Krisheim, on what is now Cresheim Creek, a tributary of the Wissahickon. Wise Mill Road, Thomas Mill Road, and Bells Mill Road, all of which lead from the highlands down to the creek at various points along the valley, perpetuate some of the other mill sites and names — although, in fact, the names of the mill owners and access roads constantly changed. (For example, in Smedley's 1862 *Atlas of the City of Philadelphia*, Thomas Mill Road is shown as Spruce Mill Lane and Bells Mill Road is Paul's Mill Lane.)

Manufacturing was Germantown's chief stimulus to growth. The area became an early printing and publishing center, and fine linen cloth produced by settlers from Krefeld on the lower

Rhine came to be well known throughout the Colonies. In addition to the textile mills were factories for processing flax for linen thread and for fulling and dyeing cloth.

At first the products of these operations were carried overland through Germantown to Philadelphia, but in 1826 a road from Rittenhouse Village to the Schuylkill River was constructed along Wissahickon Creek. In 1856 the Wissahickon Turnpike Company completed its road (now Forbidden Drive) running the entire length of the valley.

Manufacturing in the Wissahickon gorge came to an end, however, when the region was acquired for Fairmount Park. By the Act of Assembly of 1868, the park commission was directed to appropriate land to the heights on either side of the valley. During the next fifteen years, all of the mills were torn down in order to protect the purity of the Schuylkill River, which was Philadelphia's water supply.

Although of secondary importance at the time, preservation of the Wissahickon scenery was also a recognized goal. Fanny Kemble, the highly praised British actress who later married (and divorced) Pierce Butler of Philadelphia, is said to have awakened Philadelphians to the beauty of the area through her poetry and prose descriptions of the valley. The story writer George Lippard romanticized the region, as did Edgar Allan Poe in a short magazine piece called "Morning on the Wissahiccon." With its cascades, cliffs, tall trees, and gorgelike valley, the Wissahickon appealed to the contemporary taste for picturesque and dramatic wilds popularized by the Hudson River school of artists and other landscape painters of the day. In 1867 Frederick Law Olmsted, who had collaborated with Calvert Vaux to design New York's Central Park, reported to the Fairmount Park Commission that "the Creek Road offers such unparalleled attractions for driving, it is so accessible and convenient of approach and can be secured at this time at a cost so moderate, that no route can at all be compared to it."

After the valley was acquired for the park, the creek road became a place for the fashionable set to see and be seen. T. A. Daly, a journalist, wrote in 1922:

[I]n a winter when the roads were white, and not too deeply covered, trim sleighs drawn by fast steppers flashed up and down the drive from Ridge Road to Chestnut Hill; and moonlight nights especially were all a jangle of silver bells. On fine afternoons from early spring until late fall the sedate carriage-folk of Germantown and Chestnut Hill in their broughams and landaus, the grand ladies shielding their complexions from the sun with tiny parasols and sitting scarsely less erect than their liveried coachmen, took the air and enjoyed the scenery with calm dignity . . . .

Expansion of the park in the Wissahickon area has continued to the present through gifts and purchases. Many of the valley trails and amenities are maintained by the efforts of the Friends of the Wissahickon. For information about the conservation programs and recreational activities of this group, write to Friends of the Wissahickon, Box 4068, Philadelphia, Pennsylvania 19118.

*PUBLIC TRANSIT:   From the intersection of Broad and South streets in downtown Philadelphia, take SEPTA bus A Express. Get off on Ridge Avenue at the bridge and dam near the southern end of Wissahickon Creek. You will know that your stop is coming when the bus leaves the Schuylkill Expressway and crosses the Schuylkill River.*

*Alternatively, approaching from the east or the west, take SEPTA bus E. From the east, you will know that your stop is coming when the bus descends steeply on Ridge Avenue; from the west, when the bus crosses the Schuylkill River.*

*As a third alternative, from Reading Terminal take the Norristown train to Wissahickon station. Follow Ridge Avenue downhill several hundred yards to the dam and bridge.*

*AUTOMOBILE: The southern end of the Wissahickon Valley is reachable from Ridge Avenue a few hundred yards northwest of the interchange linking Ridge with City Avenue (Route 1), East River Drive, and Wissahickon Drive. A small*

*parking lot is located on the west side of Ridge Avenue next to the bridge over Wissahickon Creek. Alternatively, park at Wissahickon station on the east side of Ridge Avenue a few hundred yards northwest of the Wissahickon Creek bridge. The entrance to the station is on a hill opposite an intersection with Cresson Street. From the station walk downhill on Ridge Avenue to Wissahickon Creek.*

*THE WALK: From the bridge and dam at the southern end of Wissahickon Creek, follow the bicycle path upstream along the left side of the valley and under a railroad bridge. On the opposite side of the valley is Wissahickon Hall, formerly a tavern and now a police station. Continue under the high bridge at Henry Avenue.*

Just before the gigantic arch of the Henry Avenue bridge is a low stone bridge leading to Hermit Lane on the left. Two taverns, the Log Cabin and the Maple Spring Hotel, once stood near the bridge on the opposite bank of the creek.

Hermit Lane recalls the sojourn in the woods of Johann Kelpius and his following of about forty men. They were German Pietists who emigrated to America in 1694 and settled near the rim of the Wissahickon Valley at the top of Hermit Lane. Calling themselves the Society of the Woman in the Wilderness, they awaited the coming of the millennium, which they believed would occur near the end of the century. They built an enormous log house — the Tabernacle of the Mystic Brotherhood — that had an observatory on its roof where they watched for the arrival of the Woman, representative of the spirit of early Christianity, which they sought to emulate in their celibacy and primitive living. Kelpius himself lived in a nearby cave. Following the death of Kelpius in 1708, his followers dispersed.

*Continue on the bicycle path as it crosses the river and hugs the bank below Wissahickon Drive. Turn left at an intersection with the broad cinder path of Forbidden Drive, where the river swerves left away from the automobile road.*

A tablet set in the rock at the trail entrance commemorates the Battle of Germantown on October 4, 1777. Part of the action took place in the lower Wissahickon Valley. The British held the southern rim of the gorge. The Pennsylvania militia under General John Armstrong were supposed to advance southward along the Schuylkill River while other columns attacked the main British force at Germantown. However, the assault was ill-coordinated and confused by fog. American and British artillery exchanged fire from the heights on each side of the valley while the opposing infantry skirmished on the lower slopes. Only a few hours after the attack began, the Americans were forced to retreat, leaving one of their cannons, in Armstrong's words, on "the horrendous hills of the Wissahickon."

*Follow the broad path along the valley and across a large masonry bridge. Keeping the creek on your right, continue on the path 2.5 miles upstream to Valley Green Inn, passing numerous intersections and several bridges along the way.*

According to one account, an inn has stood at Valley Green since 1683. The present building was built in 1850 after the previous tavern burned.

*To return downstream on the opposite side of the valley, cross the creek on the bridge just upstream from Valley Green Inn. Bear right immediately onto a wide gravel path marked with white paint blazes. Follow the path uphill, then down across a small stream and straight uphill on the far side. Turn right at a T-intersection and continue along the side of the valley. Join an asphalt road and follow it left 100 yards uphill, then turn right onto a dirt road. Follow a narrow, rough path through the woods. Turn left above a large sewer pipe so as to continue on the white-blazed trail. At a gravel road, turn left for 20 yards, then right onto a bridle path. Continue through the woods to a large clearing. Pass to the right of a riding ring. Bear right at a small corral on the far side of the Monastery Stables.*

Joseph Gorgas, a Seventh Day Baptist, bought this property in the mid-1700s and built (or at least greatly enlarged) the house for use as a monastery. Baptisms by immersion took place in Wissahickon Creek. Eventually Gorgas's followers and later Gorgas himself withdrew to the larger semimonastic community of Seventh Day Baptists at Ephrata, Pennsylvania.

*After passing to the right of the Monastery Stables, follow the gravel road downhill and along the river's edge. At a T-intersection turn right onto a bridge across Wissahickon Creek. Turn left downstream onto Forbidden Drive. Return to Ridge Avenue by the way you came.*

**5**

# WISSAHICKON VALLEY
## Northern Section

*Walking and ski touring — 4 miles (6.4 kilometers). From Bells Mill Road to Valley Green on a winding carriage road that is closed to motor vehicles. The route follows the bottom of the gorge next to Wissahickon Creek. Return on a bridle path along the side of the valley. The entire distance is through deep woods. Managed by the Fairmount Park Commission (686-2176 or 686-2177).*

---

$T$O ENTHUSIASTS OF GEOLOGY, *Wissahickon* is more than just the peculiar name of a Philadelphia creek: it identifies a massive formation of crystalline rock extending in a broad band from Trenton, through Philadelphia, across southeastern Pennsylvania, and into Delaware and eastern Maryland. It was at Wissahickon Creek, where the stream valley has cut deeply into bedrock, that the geologic unit called the Wissahickon Formation was first studied and described.

In Philadelphia the boundary between the Piedmont Plateau and the Coastal Plain is defined largely by the zone where the hard crystalline bedrock of the Wissahickon Formation dips southeastwardly beneath the thick blanket of Coastal Plain clay, silt, sand, and gravel. At Tinicum (discussed in Chapter 1) the surface of the Wissahickon bedrock protrudes upward through the silt and sand at a few points to form incongruous hills, such as Tinicum Island, within the Coastal Plain. A dozen miles to the north, the Wissahickon rocks form the dramatic highlands of Roxborough, Chestnut Hill, and Germantown. Although Wis-

sahickon Creek, flowing south from the elevated plateau of Montgomery County, has carved a deep valley through the formation, the band of crystalline rock is nonetheless more resistant to erosion than are the materials farther downstream. In consequence, cascades and rapids have developed where streams cross the Wissahickon Formation, as is characteristic of the Fall Zone between the Piedmont and Coastal Plain. For example, rapids used to occur on the Schuylkill River in the vicinity of Manayunk before the river was dammed to harness the Schuylkill's power. As discussed in Chapter 4, Wissahickon Creek similarly powered a series of mills.

Most of the rocks that the Wissahickon Formation comprises are metamorphic in origin, meaning they resulted from the application of great heat and pressure to previously existing rocks. Wissahickon schist, for example, was formed by the compression of sedimentary shale, which had been created earlier by the deposition and consolidation of mud. Wissahickon schist reflects its sedimentary origin by occurring in distinct layers that were laid down as horizontal beds. Later the beds of shale were tilted and folded by movements in the earth's crust. The pressure that caused this deformation probably also caused the sedimentary shale to change into schist, which is by far the most abundant type of rock within the Wissahickon Formation. The widespread occurrence of schist indicates that the immense pressure exerted within the bedrock occurred on a regional scale.

One result of the application of heat or pressure is recrystallization: the formation of mineral crystals larger than and sometimes chemically different from those that previously existed in the rock. Shale is made of very small mineral fragments, but schist has visible flaky crystals composed of minerals different from those found in shale. The crystals in schist are highly foliated, meaning that they occur in parallel sheets formed at right angles to the direction from which pressure was applied. The foliation produces a marked cleavage along which the rock splits apart. The tendency of crystals to reorient and adjust to directional pressure is more marked in some minerals than in

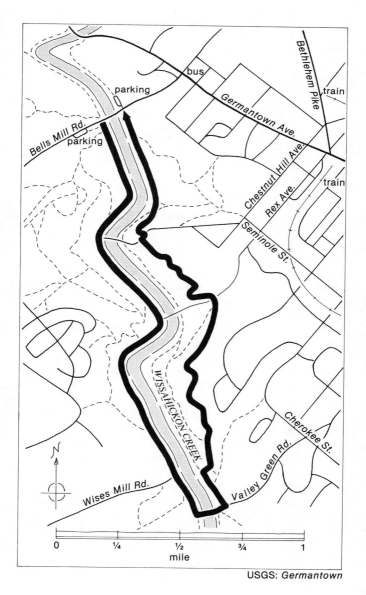

USGS: *Germantown*

47

others. Mica, for example, readily reorients to pressure; in the Wissahickon Valley the schist commonly contains shiny, flat crystals of mica. Also, many outcroppings of schist are peppered with dark-red, nearly round crystals of garnet.

Wissahickon gneiss, with crystals larger than schist, results from the metamorphosis of igneous rocks. Mobilized by pressure or heat, the minerals have reorganized themselves into distinct light and dark bands of different composition. Gneiss is harder than schist and does not show marked foliation or cleavage.

Quartzite, harder still than gneiss, is another metamorphic rock commonly found in the Wissahickon Formation. This dense rock, usually white, is recrystallized sandstone, originally formed by the deposition and cementing of sand. Like gneiss, quartzite lacks foliation or cleavage. The recrystallized grains interlock like joints of a jigsaw puzzle.

Various igneous rocks also occur within the Wissahickon Formation. Pegmatite and granite are both light-colored igneous rocks that on close examination have a coarse-grained, speckled quality. Their large crystals and lack of foliation reflect the gradual cooling of molten material called *magma* before it reached the surface of the ground. There are, however, other processes by which a sedimentary or metamorphic rock can be altered by heat or pressure so that it becomes pegmatite or granite, as may have occurred at places in the Wissahickon Valley.

Pegmatite has particularly large crystals. Quartz, mica, and feldspar can be seen easily, often in crystals ½ inch across or larger. As an igneous rock, pegmatite usually occurs in thin veins called *sills* that penetrated as magma between beds of sedimentary rock. Pegmatite also occurs as so-called *dikes* cutting across the grain of the surrounding rock, perhaps as a result of flowing through joints in the stone. Sometimes *xenoliths* (literally, "foreign rocks") are embedded within the pegmatite. They are sedimentary or metamorphic fragments that were enveloped by the igneous intrusion.

The occurrence of alternating layers of schist and quartzite, all of which have been tilted, folded, and intermixed with other metamorphic and igneous rocks, suggests a scenario for the creation of the Wissahickon Formation. It appears that the Wissahickon zone was covered by a shallow sea in which beds of mud and sand were deposited one after another. That, at any rate, is the type of environment in which mud and sand are deposited today. As the sediments accumulated they were compacted by their own weight and cemented to form shale and sandstone. Then a period of regional compression from the southeast and northwest crumpled the beds of sedimentary rock and changed the shale and sandstone to schist and quartzite. At the same time, intrusions of magma penetrated through faults and fissures in the rock. Erosion has subsequently dissected the formation and exposed the rocks to view. This entire process may have been part of the sequence of sediment accumulation, regional compression, and erosion that occurred between 600 million and 225 million years ago, which produced the Appalachian Mountains we know today. Or, the Wissahickon Formation may have been created during an earlier period.

In the course of your walk in the Wissahickon Valley, examine the stone outcroppings that occur frequently along the path, stream, and slopes to see if you can observe any of the rock types and formations described above. For enthusiasts, Bruce K. Goodwin's *Guidebook to the Geology of the Philadelphia Area,* published by the Pennsylvania Geological Survey, provides a detailed discussion of dozens of specific sites within the valley.

*PUBLIC TRANSIT: From Olney station near the northern end of the Broad Street subway line, walk half a block north to Chew Avenue. From there take SEPTA bus L, which eventually travels north on Germantown Avenue. Get off at the intersection with Bells Mill Road. You will know that your stop is coming after the bus passes through Chestnut Hill. From the bus stop walk west downhill on Bells Mill Road for*

⅓ mile to Forbidden Drive on the west side of Wissahickon Creek.

Alternatively, from Reading Terminal take the train to Chestnut Hill East. From the station follow Chestnut Hill Avenue southwest ⅔ mile to an intersection with Seminole Street. Turn right onto the footpath leading downhill into the woods. Use the map to pick up the trail circuit.

As a third alternative, take the train from Penn Center, 30th Street station, or North Philadelphia to Chestnut Hill West. From the station follow Germantown Avenue north two blocks. Turn left onto Chestnut Hill Avenue and go ½ mile to an intersection with Seminole Street. Turn right onto a footpath leading downhill into the woods. Use the map to pick up the trail circuit.

AUTOMOBILE:   From the interchange linking Ridge Avenue, City Avenue (Route 1), East River Drive, and Wissahickon Drive, follow Ridge Avenue northwest almost 5 miles to Bells Mill Road. Turn right onto Bells Mill Road and follow it downhill. Park either in a large lot on the right 0.1 mile from the bottom of the valley or in another lot on the east side of Wissahickon Creek.

Alternatively, from Chestnut Hill, where Bethlehem Pike joins Germantown Avenue, go north 0.7 mile on Germantown Avenue. Turn left onto Bells Mill Road and follow it to the bottom of the valley. Park in the lot on the right just before the bridge over Wissahickon Creek.

THE WALK:   From the Bells Mill bridge over Wissahickon Creek, follow the wide cinder path of Forbidden Drive downstream along the west side of the river. Keeping the creek on your left, continue past numerous side trails and three bridges to Valley Green Inn, 2 miles distant. The first bridge downstream from Bells Mill Road is a covered bridge built in 1855.

To return on the opposite side of the valley, cross the creek on the bridge just upstream from Valley Green Inn. Turn left at the end of the stone parapet onto a footpath marked with white paint blazes. Fork left to cross a small stream, then climb right to rejoin the white-blazed trail about 40 yards from the edge of Wissahickon Creek. Follow the trail as it climbs and dips along the side of the valley. Cross a rocky road. Continue on the white-blazed path as it climbs first left, then sharply to the right, then left again before passing above a giant statue of a crouched Indian, carved by Massey Rhind in 1902. The stone statue at Indian Rock replaces an earlier wood statue erected in 1854.

At a T-intersection with another road, bear right uphill for 50 yards, then turn left on the white-blazed footpath. Curve around and down to the right. Continue straight through an oblique four-way intersection. Return along the edge of the creek to Bells Mill Road.

# 6

# SCHUYLKILL VALLEY
# NATURE CENTER

*Walking — 1 or more miles (1.6 or more kilometers). A private nature preserve of 500 acres. Six miles of foot trails lead through meadows, weedy fields, and wooded ravines where the Upper Roxborough highlands slope toward the Schuylkill River. Here you can see deer within the city limits. Open Monday through Saturday from 8:30 A.M. to 5:00 P.M.; Sunday from 1:00 to 5:00 P.M. Closed Sundays in August and major holidays. A small admission fee is charged. Dogs and picnicking are prohibited. Managed by the Schuylkill Valley Nature Center for Environmental Education, Inc. (482-7300).*

---

THE LARGE TRACT of fields and woods at the Schuylkill Valley Nature Center probably has changed less during the last three centuries than any other area of comparable size in Philadelphia. Even the Wissahickon and Pennypack valleys have seen the development and demise of numerous mills and quarries. Fairmount Park, crisscrossed with roads and dotted with eighteenth-century mansions, nineteenth-century monuments, and twentieth-century recreational and cultural amenities, tells its own story of change. But the land at the Schuylkill Valley Nature Center, from the time of William Penn to the establishment of the nature preserve in 1965, was simply farmland. Now much of the area has reverted to woods, presumably as it was before the first European settlers arrived.

Traces of the farms remain. Ruined springhouses and a small, decrepit bank barn are set into the bluff. Several farmhouses are

*Common Milkweed,* Asclepias syriaca

occupied by staff members of the nature center. Old aerial photographs show that as late as 1936 most of the property was still fields. The last farming was a dairy operation, which ceased in 1957. Now some of the fields are kept clear by periodic mowing and burning in order to provide a variety of wildlife habitats.

In 1694 the land that is now the preserve was included in a grant from William Penn to several of his creditors, including Isaac Norris, whose name was later given to Norristown. During the following two centuries the property was divided into many parcels that were reassembled in 1886, when Henry Howard Houston acquired the entire tract. A director of the Pennsylvania Railroad and an investor in Pennsylvania oil fields and western gold mines, Houston bought a vast area on both sides of the Wissahickon Valley. For the next seventy years his family held the tract that was later to become the nature center, leasing it to farmers. In 1946 the United Nations almost purchased the property as the site of its headquarters, but at the last moment, while the Houston family representatives were on the train to New York to consummate the transaction, John D. Rockefeller, Jr., scotched the deal by offering the United Nations $8.5 million to buy land bordering the East River in New York. Twenty years later the Houstons sold the property for a nominal price to the newly organized Schuylkill Valley Nature Center, a nonprofit corporation.

Concentrating on environmental education, the nature center conducts a wide variety of programs and field trips for schoolchildren, teachers, senior citizens, handicapped persons, and the general public. The center's headquarters contain a bookstore, a library, an auditorium, and classrooms. Family events are offered every weekend. For information telephone the headquarters or write to the Schuylkill Valley Nature Center, 8480 Hagy's Mill Road, Philadelphia, Pennsylvania 19128.

*PUBLIC TRANSIT: From the intersection of Broad and South streets in downtown Philadelphia, take SEPTA bus A Express. From North Philadelphia take the A Local. Eventu-*

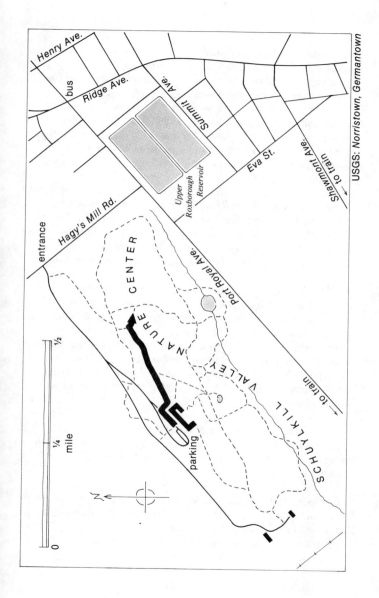

USGS: *Norristown, Germantown*

Henry Ave.

bus

Ridge Ave.

Summit Ave.

Upper Roxborough Reservoir

Eva St.

Shawmont Ave.

to train

Hagy's Mill Rd.

entrance

CENTER

Port Royal Ave.

NATURE

VALLEY

SCHUYLKILL

to train

parking

½    ¼    0
mile

N

55

*ally these two buses follow Ridge Avenue — or in some instances, Henry Avenue. In either case get off at the intersection with Port Royal Avenue. You will know that your stop is coming after the bus passes Summit Avenue.*

*From the bus stop walk west on Port Royal Avenue past a playground on the right and the old Upper Roxborough Reservoir on the left. Turn right onto Hagy's Mill Road and go 0.3 mile to the entrance to the Schuylkill Valley Nature Center on the left. Take the footpath that veers left just inside the gate. This path soon joins the larger trail system.*

*The Nature Center also can be reached by taking the Norristown train from Reading Terminal. Get off at Shawmont. Follow Shawmont Avenue 0.8 mile uphill to Eva Street. Turn left and follow Eva Street 0.5 mile to Port Royal Avenue. Turn right onto Port Royal, then left onto Hagy's Mill Road. Continue 0.3 mile to the Nature Center entrance.*

*AUTOMOBILE: The Schuylkill Valley Nature Center is located near Ridge Avenue in Upper Roxborough, about 4 miles northwest of the intersection linking Ridge Avenue, City Avenue (Route 1), East River Drive, and Wissahickon Drive. Follow Ridge Avenue northwest to Port Royal Avenue. Turn left onto Port Royal and go 0.2 mile. Turn right onto Hagy's Mill Road and continue 0.3 mile to the entrance to the Nature Center on the left. Follow the drive and signs to the parking area.*

*THE WALK: Facing the front of the visitor center, circle left around the building to an asphalt path. Follow the path left to a bird blind. From there continue clockwise through the trail system.*

As indicated by the presence of the Upper Roxborough Reservoir and the water towers to the north, the intersection of Ridge and Port Royal avenues near the Schuylkill Valley Nature Center is one of the highest spots in Philadelphia.

An earlier name for Port Royal Avenue was Ship Lane. During the late eighteenth century many wealthy families established rural retreats in the highlands north of Philadelphia in order to escape the yellow fever that plagued the city each summer. The servants of shipowners were supposedly sent to the summit at Ship Lane to determine, with the aid of a spyglass, which vessels — identifiable by the distinctive pennants that they flew — had come into port. Upon learning that his ship literally had come in, the happy owner could then make the day's trip into the city.

At 8232 Ridge Avenue, just south of the intersection with Port Royal Avenue, mile post 9 on the old Ridge Road still marks the point where a bizarre Revolutionary War episode occurred. Here, on May 20, 1778, a detachment of Continental Light Dragoons and Oneida Indians encountered a column of British Light Horse advancing from Philadelphia. What were the Indians doing there? The Oneidas were the only tribe among the Six Nations of the Iroquois Confederacy who had allied themselves with the patriot cause instead of the British. They had been recruited at the suggestion of General Washington, who thought that Indians would be valuable as scouts and light troops. Although Washington later changed his mind because he did not want to sponsor what he called the "irregularities" of Indian-style warfare, a contingent of Oneidas from central New York nonetheless reached Valley Forge on May 13, 1778, creating something of a stir. Two days later the Chevalier de Pontgibaud, a French volunteer, wrote:

While some French officers were at dinner with his Excellency [General Washington] an Indian soldier entered the room, walked around the table, and then stretched forth his long tattooed arm and seized a large joint of hot roast beef in his thumb and fingers, took it to the door, and began to eat it. Genl Washington gave orders that he was not to be interfered with, saying laughingly, that it was apparently the dinner hour of this *Mutius Scaevola* of the New World. [Mutius Scaevola was a roman consul and pontifex maximus. In

57

Colonial America the Iroquois tribes were compared to the Romans because of their sophisticated political system and military prowess.]

A few days later the Indians were among a force of over two thousand troops assembled for an expedition toward Philadelphia, which the British had occupied the previous fall. Now rumors had reached Valley Forge that an evacuation of the city was imminent. The purpose of the American foray was to ascertain the facts and to pursue and harass the British if they abandoned Philadelphia.

Led by Major General Lafayette, the American troops left Valley Forge after midnight on May 19. On the following morning they reached Barren Hill at mile post 12 on the Ridge Road. "We halted here, placed our guards, sent off our scouting parties, and waited for — I know not what," wrote one soldier:

A company of about a hundred Indians, from some northern tribe, joined us here. There were three or four young Frenchmen with them. The Indians were stout-looking fellows and remarkably neat for that race of mortals, but they were Indians. There was upon the hill, and just where we were lying, an old church built of stone, entirely divested of all its entrails. The Indians were amusing themselves and the soldiers by shooting with their bows, in and about the church. I observed something in a corner of the roof which did not appear to belong to the building, and desired an Indian who was standing near me to shoot an arrow at it. He did so and it proved to be a cluster of bats; I should think there were nearly a bushel of them, all hanging upon one another. The house was immediately alive with them, and it was likewise instantly full of Indians and soldiers. The poor bats fared hard; it was sport for all hands. They killed I know not how many, but there was a great slaughter among them. I never saw so many bats before nor since, nor indeed in my whole life put all together.

That night the troops bivouacked at Barren Hill. The British, however, had learned of the American expedition, and after dark more than five thousand British soldiers left Philadelphia. By a roundabout route, two columns approached Barren Hill from the north and east while a third column advanced directly from the south. On the Ridge Road, the British Light Horse ran into the American vanguard at mile post 9. According to one observer, "The Indians war-whooped and the British as well as the Indians departed the field, the latter discharging their pieces at the Light Horse. Terrified, the British Horse scampered off and the Indians collected some cloaks which the Enemy had dropped in his flight."

One of the American dragoons at the outpost carried the news back to the main force at Barren Hill, where Lafayette already had learned of the other enemy columns approaching from the east and north. With only a few casualties, the Americans quickly retreated to safety across the Schuylkill River. As for the Indians: "They kept coming in all the afternoon, in parties of four or five, whooping and hallooing like wild beasts," wrote the soldier who had witnessed the battle of the bats the day before. "After they had got collected they vanished; I never saw any more of them. Our scouting parties all came in safe, but I was afterwards informed by a British deserter that several of the enemy perished by the heat and their exertions to get away from a retreating enemy."

On June 13 an ensign from New York was assigned the task of supervising the journey north of thirty-five of the Oneidas who, said Washington, "are desirous of returning home."

# 7

# MORRIS ARBORETUM

*Walking — 1 or more miles (1.6 or more kilometers). A magnificent country estate planted with thousands of varieties of native and exotic trees and shrubs. The Morris mansion is gone, but the lawns, ponds, formal gardens, and other landscape features remain. Open daily 9:00 A.M. to 5:00 P.M., April through October; 9:00 A.M. to 4:00 P.M., November through March. A small admission fee is charged. Dogs must be leashed. Picnicking is prohibited. Managed by the University of Pennsylvania (247-5777).*

---

**T**HE MORRIS ARBORETUM in Chestnut Hill is more than just a collection of trees and shrubs assembled for scientific study and propagation. It is also an elaborately landscaped and meticulously maintained country estate of the late nineteenth century, reflecting the affluence, taste, and enthusiasm of its former owners, John T. Morris and his sister Lydia. With the exuberance of wealth, the Morrises adorned their country seat with a wide variety of traditional landscape features, including Italian fountains and balustraded overlooks, an English park, a terrace rose garden, an oak *allée*, an azalea meadow, and a swan pond and Tuscan love temple.

John and Lydia Morris began to develop Compton (as they called their estate) in 1887, six years after John had retired from active management of his family's various ironworks in Pennsylvania and New Jersey. A baronial stone mansion was built at the top of the hill but later torn down. The large masonry structure that remains at the edge of the woods above Wissahickon Creek is merely the former carriage house. John Mor-

*Oak allée*

ris died in 1915 and Lydia in 1931, bequeathing their 175-acre estate to the University of Pennsylvania for use as an arboretum and research center.

The Morrises had a particularly strong interest in Oriental horticulture. They traveled to Japan and hired Japanese gardeners to work at Compton in their own tradition. Also, the Morrises were friends of Professor Charles Sprague Sargent and Ernest ''Chinese'' Wilson at Harvard University's Arnold Arboretum. Wilson was a plant explorer who in the late 1800s brought many Oriental seeds and seedlings to America. Now fully grown, some of these specimens can be seen at the Morris Arboretum.

Today the arboretum has over thirty-five hundred varieties of trees and shrubs from the north temperate zone around the world. Each is labeled with a metal tag attached to the trunk or a branch, listing the plant's scientific and common names and its natural range. The Morris Arboretum is thus a perfect place to learn about both native and foreign plants, or just to go for a stroll in a beautiful setting.

Learning to identify trees is not difficult. Every walk or automobile trip is an opportunity for practice. Notice the overall forms and branching habits of the trees, and also the distinctive qualities of their twigs, buds, bark, leaves, flowers, and fruits or seeds, which are the key identification features distinguishing one species from another. Finally, when using a field guide, check the maps or descriptions that delineate the geographic range within which the tree or shrub is likely to be found.

Some trees, of course, have very distinctive and reliable forms. Familiar evergreens like Balsam Fir and Red Cedar have a conical shape, like a dunce cap, although in dense stands the Red Cedar tapers very little and assumes the columnar form of the Italian Cypress, which it somewhat resembles. The deciduous Little-leaf Linden, imported from Europe and used as a street tree, is more or less conical. Elm displays a spreading form like a head of broccoli. A full-bodied egg-shape is characteristic of Sugar Maples and beeches, although both will develop long, branchless trunks in crowded woods, as do most

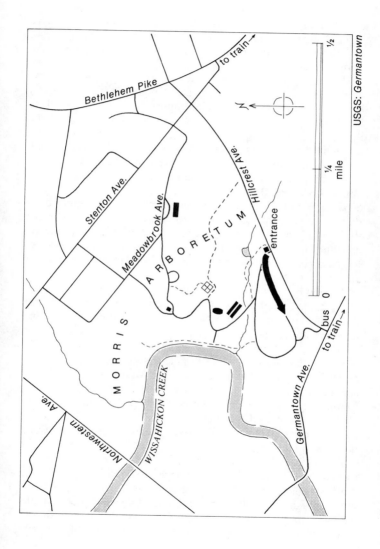

forest trees competing for light. The vertically exaggerated cigar shape of Lombardy Poplars — a form called fastigiate — and the pendulous, trailing quality of Weeping Willows are unmistakable.

Branching habit, an important clue to some trees, is observable even at a distance. White Pine, for example, has markedly horizontal branches with a slight upward tilt at the tips, like a hand palm upward. Norway Spruce, usually seen as an ornamental tree dwarfing and darkening a house near which it was planted fifty or a hundred years ago, is a very tall evergreen with long, evenly spaced, drooping lower branches. The slender lower branches of Pin Oak slant downward, while those of White Oak and Red Oak often are massive and horizontal, especially on trees growing in the open. The lower branches of the Horse Chestnut (another European import) also droop but then curl up at the tips in chunky twigs. Elm branches spread up and out like the mouth of a trumpet. The trunk of the Honeylocust diverges into large branches, somewhat in the manner of an American Elm.

A good botanist or nursery worker can identify trees by their twigs alone, that is, by the end portion of the branch that constitutes the newest growth. During winter the shape, color, size, position, and sheathing of the buds are important. For instance, beech buds are long and pointed, tan, and sheathed with overlapping scales like shingles. Sycamore and magnolia buds are wrapped in a single scale. The twigs of Horse Chestnut are tipped with a big, sticky, brown bud, while those of Silver Maple, and to a lesser extent of Red Maple, end with large clusters of red buds. Some oaks, such as White Oak, have hairless terminal buds, while other species, such as Black Oak, have hairy end buds.

Aside from buds, other characteristics of twigs are color, thorns, hair, pith, and the size, shape, and position of leaf scars marking where the leaf stems were attached. For example, most maple twigs are reddish brown, but the twigs of Striped Maple and Mountain Maple are greenish. Thorns and spines are significant because relatively few trees have them, notably Honeylocust, Black Locust, Hercules Club, Prickly Ash, Buckthorn Bumelia, Devil's-walkingstick, Osage-orange, American Plum, some crab apples, and the many varieties of hawthorn. Most oaks have hairless twigs, although some species such as Blackjack Oak are distinctly hairy. As for pith, it can be chambered, solid, spongy, or of different colors depending on the species. Oak, hickory, and Tulip-trees are common forest species near Philadelphia, yet of the three only the twigs of Tulip-trees have chambered pith, while the pith of White Oak in cross section forms a star. Finally, in winter the location of leaf scars in opposite pairs along the twigs (as with maples) distinguishes a wide variety of trees and shrubs from those with leaf scars arranged alternately, first on one side and then the other (as with oaks). All these distinguishing features can best be appreciated simply by examining the twigs of different species.

Bark is not always a reliable clue, as its color and texture often change with age or from trunk to branches to twigs. Often the distinctive character of bark is seen only in the trunks of large, mature trees. Bark can be smooth, furrowed, scaly, plated, shaggy, fibrous, crisscrossed, corky, or papery. Some trees, of course, are unmistakable because of their bark. The names Shagbark Hickory and Paper Birch (a northern species not found near Philadelphia) speak for themselves. Striped Maple has longitudinal, whitish stripes in the smooth green bark of the younger trees. The crisscrossed ridges of White Ash, the light blotches on Sycamores, and the smooth gray skin of beech are equally distinctive. Birches and some cherries are characterized by horizontal lenticels like random dashes.

Everybody notices leaves. Most obvious is the overall shape. Gray Birch is triangular, Catalpa heart-shaped, Sweetgum star-shaped, beech elliptical (or actually pointed at each end), and Black Willow narrower still and thus "lanceolate." Notice also the leaf margin or edge. Is it smooth like rhododendron, wavy like Water Oak, serrated like basswood, or deeply lobed like most maples? And how many lobes are there? Tulip-trees, for example, have easily recognized, four-lobed leaves; maples have three- or five-lobed leaves. Also are the lobe tips rounded like White Oak or pointed like Red Oak? Or maybe, as with Sassafras and Red Mulberry, the same tree has differently shaped leaves, the most distinctive being those with a single, asymmetrical lobe creating a leaf outline like a mitten.

Some leaves such as Japanese Maple, Horse Chestnut, and Ohio Buckeye are palmately compound, meaning that they are actually composed of leaflets radiating from the end of the stem like fingers from the palm. In the fall the whole compound leaf drops off the tree as a unit. Other leaves, such as ash, hickory, and sumac, are pinnately compound, being composed of leaflets arranged in pairs along a central stalk. Still other leaves are *bi*-pinnately compound, somewhat like a fern. The leaflets grow from stalks that in turn spread from a central stalk. Honeylocust, Kentucky Coffeetree, and the ornamental imported Silktree are examples.

Although the needles of evergreens are not as varied as the leaves of deciduous plants, there are still several major points to look for, such as the number of needles grouped together. White Pine has fascicles of five; Pitch Pine, Loblolly Pine, and sometimes Shortleaf Pine have fascicles of three; and Red Pine, Virginia Pine, Austrian Pine, and sometimes Shortleaf Pine have fascicles of two. Needles of spruce, hemlock, and fir grow singly, but are joined to the twig in distinctive ways. Spruce needles grow from little woody pegs, hemlock needles from smaller bumps, and fir needles directly from the twig, leaving a rounded pit when pulled off. Spruce needles tend to be four-sided, hemlock flat, and fir somewhere in between. Larch needles (which all drop off in winter) grow in dense clusters.

Flowers are a spectacular though short-lived feature of some trees and shrubs. Three variables are color, form, and (less reliably) time of bloom. Redbud, with red-purple clusters, and Shadbush (also called Allegheny Serviceberry), with small, white, five-petaled flowers, are among the first of our native eastern trees to bloom, perhaps as early as late March near Philadelphia. In April comes dogwood. The blossoms of Flowering Dogwood consist of four white, petal-like bracts, each with a brown notch at the tip, while the flowers of Alternate-leaf

*American Beech*, Fagus grandifolia

Dogwood consist of loose white clusters. Mountain Laurel and rhododendron bloom in late spring and early summer. These are a few of our native species commonly thought of as flowering trees and shrubs, but the blossoms of other native species are equally distinctive, such as the small but numerous flowers of maples or the tulip-like flowers and durable husks of Tulip-trees. Also, at the Morris Arboretum the cycle of bloom is enriched by various foreign trees, including the early-flowering Japanese Dogwood and some varieties of magnolia and Oriental cherries.

Finally, the seeds or fruit of a tree are a conspicuous element in summer and fall, sometimes lasting into winter and even spring. Nobody who sees a tree with acorns could fail to know that it is an oak, although some varieties, such as Willow Oak, are otherwise deceptive. Distinctive nuts are also produced by beech trees, Horse Chestnut, hickories, and walnut. Some seeds, like ash and maple, have wings. Others, such as Honey-locust, Kentucky Coffeetree, and Redbud, come in pods like beans and in fact are members of the same general legume family. The seeds of birches, poplars, and willows hang in tassels, while those of Sweetgum and sycamore form prickle-balls (as do the shells of Horse Chestnut and buckeye). And, of course, brightly colored berries and fruits are produced by many species, such as holly, hawthorn, and hackberry. Among needle evergreens, spruce and pine cones hang from the twigs, while fir cones stand upright, and the small hemlock cones grow from the twig tips.

*PUBLIC TRANSIT:    From Olney station near the northern end of the Broad Street subway line, walk half a block north to Chew Avenue. From there take SEPTA bus L, which eventually travels north on Germantown Avenue. Get off at the intersection with Hillcrest Avenue on the right. You will know that your stop is coming after the bus goes through Chestnut Hill and past Bells Mill Road. From the bus stop walk east on Hillcrest Avenue 0.2 mile to the entrance to the Morris Arboretum on the left.*

Alternatively, from Reading Terminal take the train to Chestnut Hill East. From the station walk north on Bethlehem Pike, then turn left onto Stenton Avenue. Follow Stenton as it curves right downhill. Turn left on Hillcrest Avenue and go 0.2 mile to the entrance to Morris Arboretum on the right.

As a third alternative, take the train from Penn Center, 30th Street station, or North Philadelphia to Chestnut Hill West. From the station walk north 1 mile on Germantown Avenue, then turn right onto Hillcrest Avenue. Continue 0.2 mile to the arboretum entrance on the left.

AUTOMOBILE: From the highway interchange linking Ridge Avenue, City Avenue (Route 1), East River Drive, and Wissahickon Drive, follow Ridge Avenue northwest 5 miles to Bells Mill Road. Turn right on Bells Mill Road and follow it down through the Wissahickon Valley and up to Germantown Avenue. Turn left on Germantown Avenue and go 0.2 mile to Hillcrest Avenue. Turn right onto Hillcrest Avenue and continue 0.2 mile to the entrance to the Morris Arboretum on the left.

Alternatively, from Chestnut Hill, where Bethlehem Pike joins Germantown Avenue, go north nearly 1 mile on Germantown Avenue to Hillcrest Avenue. Turn right onto Hillcrest Avenue and go 0.2 mile to the entrance to the Morris Arboretum on the left.

THE WALK: At the Hillcrest Avenue gatehouse pick up one of the excellent arboretum maps. Start your walk by forking left toward the Japanese Garden and English Park. Gradually circle right to tour the rest of the arboretum.

If you want to extend your walk beyond the main body of the arboretum, you can explore the large overgrown meadow bordering Wissahickon Creek north of the central hill.

**8**

# PENNYPACK CREEK
## Southern Section

*Walking and ski touring — 8 miles (12.9 kilometers). A linear park cutting across northeastern Philadelphia. Drop out of the city into a quiet, wooded valley. Follow bicycle paths and horse trails next to Pennypack Creek. Managed by the Fairmount Park Commission (686-2176 or 686-2177).*

---

BEFORE AMERICAN INDUSTRY converted from water power to steam during the nineteenth century, Pennypack Creek (like Wissahickon Creek) was the site of a chain of water-driven mills and factories, recalled now by the names of various roads. In the Holmesburg section of Philadelphia there is Mill Street, site of several old factories. Farther upstream are Axe Factory Road and Verree Road (after Robert Verree and his descendants, owners of a small mill complex). In Montgomery County are Fetter's Mill Road, Paper Mill Road, Mill Road, and Saw Mill Lane. The first recorded mills were erected in the late seventeenth century, but there may have been earlier, unrecorded mills built by the Swedish settlers who preceded the establishment of Penn's colony. By one estimate about thirty-five mills were powered by Pennypack Creek and its tributaries in the early 1800s, including gristmills, sawmills, fulling mills, linseed oil mills, powder mills, shovel works, and other factories.

Smedley's 1862 *Atlas of the City of Philadelphia* shows ten mills along the portion of Pennypack Creek within the municipal boundaries. At Holmesburg — at that time separated from the center of Philadelphia by open farmland — there were Pennock's Grist and Saw Mill, Jonathan Large & Brothers'

*Holmesburg dam*

Cotton Factory, and an "old saw mill," all on the west bank downstream from the bridge of the Bristol Turnpike (i.e., Frankford Avenue). The Holmesburg dam still stands above the bridge. The remains of a mill race — now a shallow trough — are discernible stretching from the west end of the dam, under Frankford Avenue, and downstream toward Torresdale Avenue.

Rowland's Shovel Works, founded in 1826, is shown in Smedley's atlas at the confluence of Pennypack Creek and Wooden Bridge Run about ¾ mile above Holmesburg. Nearby was a gristmill, and upstream above Welsh Road was the small factory community — including the mill and about eighteen houses — of Andrew Hartel & Company's Pennypack Print Works, where calico was bleached, dyed, and printed. Still intact, the Hartel dam is located upstream from the lower Rhawn Street bridge. Rowland's and Hartel's were large operations. The former employed fifty hands and the latter one hundred fifty hands by the late 1800s, when both factories were powered by steam as well as water.

A photograph of Hartel's factory in about 1910 shows not only a substantial mill building but also a valley covered with scrubby, immature forest. During the eighteenth and early nineteenth centuries, when wood was the only fuel for cooking and heating, the valley probably was stripped of trees, with pastures sloping down to the creek.

Other mills included in Smedley's atlas are Lathrop's Cotton Factory in LaGrange, a small community of about two dozen houses clustered near Pennypack Creek at the Bustleton Pike bridge. At Krewstown Road (shown as Krenstone Lane) there was the Walnut Mill, and about ½ mile upstream, Prince's Mill. J. P. Verree's mill community of Verreeville, where axes, hatchets, and shovels were made, was located where Verree Road crosses the creek.

By the beginning of the twentieth century, when the 8-mile stretch of Pennypack Valley within Philadelphia was acquired by the Fairmount Park Commission, most of the Pennypack mills had been abandoned. The rise of steam power freed manufacturers from the need to locate their factories in narrow

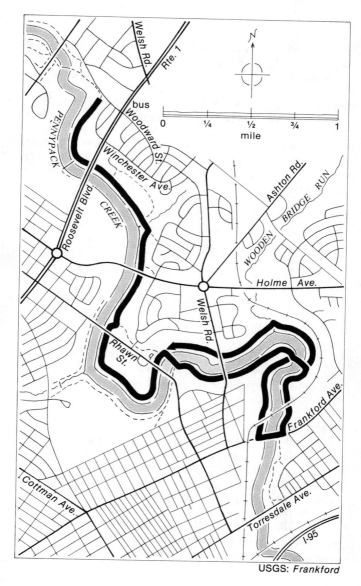

USGS: *Frankford*

73

stream valleys, where the works were subject to periodic flooding and had poor access to navigable waterways. Also, the shift in wheat cultivation from the eastern states to the northern Great Plains and beyond doomed the many small gristmills of the mid-Atlantic region. Those factories which remained in the Pennypack Valley in the early 1900s, such as Rowland's Shovel Works and Hartel's Pennypack Print Works, were purchased by the city starting in 1905 and eventually torn down. Now the chief relics of the various Pennypack mills are an occasional dam along the steam in a valley that has otherwise reverted to deep woods.

*PUBLIC TRANSIT:    From Bridge-Pratt Terminal at the eastern end of the Market-Frankford subway line, take SEPTA bus B east on Roosevelt Boulevard. Get off at the intersection with Woodward Street. You will know that your stop is coming after the bus crosses the wooded valley of Pennypack Creek and then passes an intersection with Winchester Avenue on the right. Approaching on bus B from the opposite direction, you will know that your stop is coming after the bus passes an intersection with Welsh Road.*

*From the bus stop walk north two blocks on Woodward Street. The park path enters the woods on the left a few dozen yards beyond the corner of Woodward Street and Winchester Avenue.*

*AUTOMOBILE:    Roosevelt Boulevard (Route 1) passes two blocks from the start of this walk. Approaching from the west, take Roosevelt Boulevard from the Schuylkill Expressway (I-76). Go slightly more than 10 miles to an intersection with Woodward Street shortly after Roosevelt Boulevard crosses the wooded Pennypack Valley. Turn left (north) onto Woodward Street and continue two blocks. Park on the left by the edge of the woods.*

*Approaching from the northeast, follow Roosevelt Boulevard past North Philadelphia Airport and an intersection*

*with Welsh Road. Three-tenths of a mile beyond the in-*
*tersection with Welsh Road, turn right onto Woodward*
*Street. Follow Woodward Street two blocks. Park on the*
*left by the edge of the woods.*

*THE WALK:   Start on the asphalt bicycle path a few dozen*
*yards north of the intersection of Woodward Street and*
*Winchester Avenue. Follow the path to the left downhill*
*into the woods and along the creek. With the stream on the*
*right, pass a footbridge and continue under the Roosevelt*
*Avenue bridge (previously called the Bensalem bridge).*
*After passing over a stone bridge, turn right. Pass a path*
*intersecting from the left and continue under the Holme*
*Avenue bridge. At a T-intersection turn right and continue*
*under Rhawn Street. Go by a dam and then under another*
*bridge where the creek again passes under Rhawn Street.*
*Andrew Hartel & Company's Pennypack Print Works stood*
*here.*

*After passing a parking lot on the left, turn right across a*
*footbridge. Continue left downstream through a picnic*
*area and past a band shell. Fork left to continue under the*
*Welsh Road bridge. Eventually cross the creek on another*
*footbridge. Continue downstream with the creek on the*
*right. Pass under a railroad bridge and by a breached dam*
*that used to provide water to a series of mills in Holmes-*
*burg. Continue to Frankford Avenue.*

The present-day Frankford Avenue bridge incorporates within its structure the original stone spans built in 1697, making it
one of the oldest bridges in the U.S. It was part of the King's
Highway linking Philadelphia and New York. Residents along
the road were required to contribute money or their own labor
toward construction and maintenance. In 1803 a tollgate was
erected at the bridge when the road became part of the Frankford
and Bristol Turnpike. The bridge was widened in 1895, so it is
not likely that any of the original stonework is visible.

75

At Frankford Avenue turn right (east) and follow the road across Pennypack Creek. Turn right back into the park. Pass through a parking area and follow the broad path between large boulders. Notice the remains of the Holmesburg mill race at the near end of the dam.

Continue upstream past the dam and back under the railroad bridge. Follow the path as it climbs, curves right along the rim of the valley, and descends. Cross a footbridge, then turn left upstream on the other side. Cross a small tributary stream (Wooden Bridge Run). If the water in Wooden Bridge Run is high, detour upstream to a safe crossing or go back to the last bridge over Pennypack Creek and return to your starting point by following the bicycle path upstream.

After crossing Wooden Bridge Run, continue through a weedy clearing, site of Rowland's Shovel Works. Pass under the Welsh Road bridge and behind the band shell on the far side of the creek. Pass an old quarry and continue to the footbridge and parking lot just downstream from Rhawn Street. With the creek on the left, return upstream along the bicycle path.

*Sensitive Fern*, Onoclea sensibilis

# 9

# PENNYPACK CREEK
## Northern Section

*Walking and ski touring — 6 miles (9.7 kilometers). Easy trails through a narrow, wooded valley. A bicycle path stretches along Pennypack Creek between the bridges at Roosevelt Boulevard and Pine Road. Return on a bridle path along the eastern bank. Shorter excursions are possible by crossing the creek at other bridges along the way. Managed by the Fairmount Park Commission (686-2176 or 686-2177).*

---

**W**HAT ORNITHOLOGICAL DISTINCTION is shared by Philadelphia, Nashville, Savannah, and Ipswich, Massachusetts? They are the only U.S. municipalities whose names have been given to birds: the Philadelphia Vireo, the Nashville Warbler, and the Savannah and "Ipswich" Sparrows. Perhaps Ipswich should be ousted from this select set, inasmuch as the American Ornithologists' Union has determined that the Ipswich bird is merely a pale race of the Savannah breed. The "Baltimore Oriole" (now demoted by the A.O.U. to a subspecies of the Northern Oriole) and the city were both named for the Lords Baltimore, the Colonial proprietors of Maryland. Mark Catesby, an eighteenth-century naturalist, called the oriole the "Baltimore-Bird" because its colors were the same as those of the Baltimores' heraldic flag.

Early ornithologists seem to have been notably casual about naming birds. Alexander Wilson (1766-1813), frequently called the "father of American ornithology," once shot a bird in a magnolia tree; hence, Magnolia Warbler for a bird whose pre-

ferred habitat is low, moist conifers. Usually, however, Wilson named birds according to the locality where his specimens were collected. He named the Nashville Warbler and the Savannah Sparrow, but not the Philadelphia Vireo, which was named by naturalist Charles Lucien Jules Laurent Bonaparte, Prince of Canino and Musignano (and nephew of Napoleon Bonaparte).

Wilson did, however, live in the Philadelphia area when he was not traveling up and down the Atlantic seaboard and along the Mississippi frontier. On several long journeys he gathered bird specimens and enrolled subscribers for his nine-volume *American Ornithology,* most of which was written in the last seven years of his life. For a brief period in 1794-1795, after he had emigrated from Scotland, Wilson lived and worked as a weaver at Joshua Sullivan's house and mill on Pennypack Creek just downstream from Pine Road. Later he was a schoolmaster near Bristol and Philadelphia. Entirely self-taught, he became an encyclopedist, bird artist, and naturalist. After his death his work was overshadowed by the superior, life-sized drawings of John James Audubon, but Wilson was in many ways the greater pioneer, depicting 264 species of birds, of which 48 were not previously known.

In addition to birds named *by* early ornithologists and explorers, there are birds named *for* them. Wilson, for example, is memorialized in the name of a petrel, a phalarope, a plover, a warbler, and also a genus of warblers. Audubon is honored by Audubon's Shearwater and "Audubon's" Warbler, a form of Yellow-rumped Warbler. There was a measure of reciprocity about this last bird name: in 1837 John Kirk Townsend, a Philadelphia ornithologist and bird collector, named "Audubon's" Warbler, and a year or two later Audubon returned the favor with Townsend's Solitaire. Then there are species named for ornithologists' wives, daughters, and relatives, as in Anna's Hummingbird and Virginia's, Lucy's, and Grace's Warblers. Some birds bear human names connected to no one in particular. Guillemot (French for "little William"), magpie (in part based on Margaret), martin ("little Mars"), and parakeet ("little Peter") are all thought to be pet names or affectionate tags that

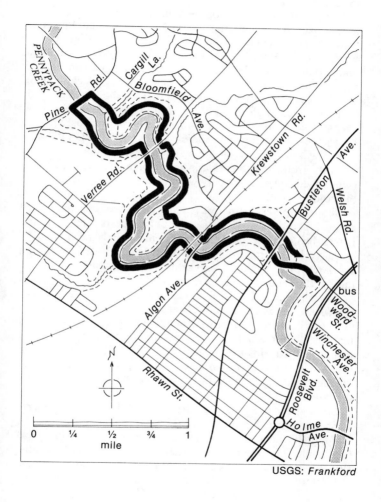

USGS: *Frankford*

81

have become attached to various species. Wherever the English have settled they have named a red-breasted bird robin.

Color is probably the dominant theme in bird names. Plumages cover the spectrum, ranging from the Red Phalarope through the Orange-crowned Warbler, Yellow Rail, Green-winged Teal, Blue Goose, Indigo Bunting, Purple Gallinule, and Violet-crowned Hummingbird. For stripped-down straightforwardness there are names like bluebird and blackbird. For grandiloquence (or is it precision?) there is the Cerulean Warbler. For meaninglessness there is the Clay-colored Sparrow. (What color is that?) Some bird names less obviously denote basic hues: vireo (green), oriole (golden), Dunlin ("little dark one"), Canvasback (for its whitish back), Brant (meaning "burnt," referring to the dark-brown plumage), and waxwing (whose red-tipped secondary wing feathers recalled to someone the color of sealing wax).

Shape or other distinctive features often are reflected in bird names. The profile of the Bufflehead suggests a buffalo. The Loggerhead Shrike has a disproportionately large head. Shovelers have long, broad bills. The word *falcon* is derived from a Latin term for "sickle," suggesting the bird's curved beak and talons. From head to toe, there is a body part that is some bird's nominal identity: Tufted Titmouse, Horned Lark, Eared Grebe (*grebe* itself may come from a Breton word for "crest"), Ruffed Grouse, Pectoral Sandpiper (for the air sack under its breast feathers), Stilt Sandpiper (for its comparatively long legs), Rough-legged Hawk (for its feathered tarsi), Sharp-shinned Hawk (it has), Semi-palmated Sandpiper (for its partially webbed feet), and Lapland Longspur (for the elongated claw on the hind toe).

Some names indicate size, from *great* and *greater* to *lesser*, *little*, and *least*. Symmetry would seem to demand a *greatest*, but perhaps that need is filled by *king*, which occasionally refers to stature. The King Rail, for example, is the largest of the rails. But sometimes *king* is simply a compliment to a bird's raiment or a reference to distinguishing plumage on its crown, as in the Ruby-crowned and Golden-crowned Kinglets ("little kings").

*Gallinule* itself suggests size, being derived from Latin for "little hen." *Starling* is from the Anglo-Saxon word for bird. With the addition of the diminutive suffix *-ling*, it simply means "little bird." *Titmouse* similarly is a combination of Icelandic and Anglo-Saxon meaning "little bird." Thus one of our most curious names has a prosaic explanation.

A few names, like that of the Gull-billed Tern, make explicit comparisons with other birds. The Lark Bunting sings on the wing like a Skylark, the Curlew Sandpiper has a downwardly curved, curlew-like bill. The Swallow-tailed Kite has a deeply forked tail like a Barn Swallow. The Turkey Vulture has a head that somewhat resembles that of a turkey. *Cormorant* is derived from French for "sea crow," and *"gannet"* is Anglo-Saxon for "little goose."

Many bird names refer to distinctive behavior. Woodpeckers, sapsuckers, creepers, and wagtails all do what their names suggest. Turnstones do indeed turn over small stones and shells while searching for food. Snipes snip and snap — the words have a common derivation. *Black Skimmer* describes the bird's technique of sticking its lower bill into the water while flying just above the surface. *Shearwater* similarly suggests the bird's skimming flight. Frigatebirds were named by sailors for the birds' piratical habit of pursuing and robbing other birds. *Duck* is derived from Anglo-Saxon for "diver." *Nuthatch* is from "nut hack," referring to the bird's occasional technique of wedging a nut into a crevice and then hacking it into small pieces. *Vulture* is from the Latin *vuellere*, "to pluck or tear." Although many people associate *loon* with the bird's lunatic laugh, as in "crazy as a loon," more likely the word is derived from a Norse term for "lame," describing the bird's awkwardness on land — a result of its legs being very near its tail. There is, however, at least one bird that is named for its mental capacity: the booby. Seamen who raided the isolated colonies thought the birds stupid because they were unaccustomed to predators and inept at protecting themselves. The Dotterel (whose name is related to "dolt" and "dotage") is another nominally foolish bird. Ernest A. Choate, in his fascinating *Dictionary of*

83

*American Bird Names,* and Edward S. Gruson, in *Words for Birds,* discuss these and other names.

Some birds, such as the Whistling Swan, Whooping Crane, Clapper Rail, Piping Plover, Laughing Gull, Mourning Dove, Warbling Vireo, and Chipping Sparrow, are named for how they sound. *Widgeon* is from a French term meaning "whistling duck." *Oldsquaw* suggests the bird's noisy, garrulous voice. The Catbird mews and the Grasshopper Sparrow trills and buzzes like the insect. Gruson, however, says that the Grasshopper Sparrow is named for its diet, as are the Goshawk ("goosehawk") and oystercatchers, flycatchers, and gnatcatchers. The Saw-whet Owl is named for the bird's endlessly repeated note, which is supposed to suggest the sound of a saw being sharpened with a whetstone. Many birds' songs or calls are also their names, including Bobolink, Bobwhite, bulbul, Chachalaca, chickadee, Chuck-will's-widow, crow, cuckoo, curlew, Dickcissel, Killdeer, kittiwake, owl, peewee, Phoebe, skua, tohwee, veery, Whimbrel (the ending is diminutive), Whip-poor-will, and Willet. *Quail* (like present-day "quack") and *raven* are thought originally to have been imitative of bird calls.

Habitat is a major theme of bird names, as in Surf Scoter, sandpiper, Sanderling ("little one of the sand"), Seaside Sparrow, Marsh Hawk, waterthrush, meadowlark, Wood Duck, bushtit, and Field, Swamp, and Tree Sparrows. Then there is the *kind* of tree or shrub, as in Spruce and Sage Grouse, Cedar Waxwing, Myrtle Warbler, Pine Siskin, and Orchard Oriole. The Tree, Bank, Cliff, and Barn swallows are named for their preferred nesting sites. As for *Prairie Warbler,* the name is simply a misnomer. Usually the bird is found in brushy, scrubby areas.

Several bird names are associated with human figures. Knots, which frequent shores and tidal flats, are said to be named for Canute (or Cnut), King of the Danes. To demonstrate to the sycophants of his court that he was not omnipotent, Canute vainly ordered the tide to stop rising. Petrels are thought to be named for Saint Peter, who walked on the water at Lake Genneserath. When landing in the water, petrels dangle their feet and hesitate for a moment, as though unsure of their ability to float. Cardinals, of course, are named for the red robes and hats of the churchmen. The bizarre and contrasting pattern of the Harlequin Duck suggests the traditional stage costume of Italian pantomime.

Finally, there is the Ovenbird, almost unique among North American birds for being named after the appearance of its nest, which is built on the forest floor and resembles a miniature Dutch oven. "Basketbird" and "hangnest" are folk names referring to the pendulous nests of orioles.

*PUBLIC TRANSIT: From Bridge-Pratt Terminal at the eastern end of the Market-Frankford subway line, take SEPTA bus B east on Roosevelt Boulevard. Get off at the intersection with Woodward Street. You will know that your stop is coming after the bus crosses the wooded valley of Pennypack Creek and then passes an intersection with Winchester Avenue on the right. Approaching on bus B from the opposite direction, you will know that your stop is coming after the bus passes an intersection with Welsh Road.*

*From the bus stop walk north two blocks on Woodward Street. The park path enters the woods on the left a few dozen yards beyond the corner of Woodward Street and Winchester Avenue.*

*AUTOMOBILE: Roosevelt Boulevard (Route 1) passes two blocks from the start of this walk. Approaching from the west, take Roosevelt Boulevard from the Schuylkill Expressway (I-76). Go slightly more than 10 miles to an intersection with Woodward Street shortly after Roosevelt Boulevard crosses the wooded Pennypack Valley. Turn left (north) onto Woodward Street and continue two blocks. Park on the left by the edge of the woods.*

*Approaching from the northeast, follow Roosevelt Boulevard past North Philadelphia Airport and an inter-*

*section with Welsh Road. Three-tenths of a mile beyond the intersection with Welsh Road, turn right onto Woodward Street. Follow Woodward Street two blocks. Park on the left by the edge of the woods.*

*THE WALK: Start on the asphalt bicycle path a few dozen yards north of the intersection of Woodward Street and Winchester Avenue. With the woods on the left, follow the path to the right along the edge of the trees, then downhill into the forest and across a bridge. With the creek on the right, continue upstream under the Bustleton Avenue bridge. Fork right to pass under the Krewstown Road bridge and then under a high railroad bridge. Eventually fork right across a bridge in order to continue along the river's edge. After 1 mile, pass through a parking lot and under the Verree Road bridge.*

The Verree Road bridge marks the site formerly occupied by Verreeville, a small mill community during the eighteenth and early nineteenth centuries. Before the American Revolution a gristmill owned by Morris Gwynne was located here. It was acquired by Robert Verree but damaged by a British raid on April 30, 1778. It is possible that the mill had been supplying flour to Continental troops. Robert Verree's son James added an axe and shovel factory. The mill dam still stands a few hundred yards upstream from the bridge. The stone Verree house is located at the eastern end of the bridge, and beyond it is the village's only remaining house for mill workers.

*With Pennypack Creek on the right, continue upstream to a grassy field by the Verree dam. Turn left away from the creek and enter the woods. Continue on the path as the creek curves alongside from the right but then curves away again. Cross a bridge and continue along the edge of a picnic area to a parking lot and Pine Road.*
*Turn right and follow Pine Road across Pennypack Creek. Thirty yards past the bridge, turn right between*

*Sassafras, Sassafras albidum*

*boulders and enter the woods on a footpath, which eventu-*
*ally fords a small tributary stream. If the water is high or*
*you are uncomfortable with this stream-crossing, return to*
*Pine Road and follow it right for several hundred yards to*
*an intersection with Bloomfield Avenue. Turn right onto*
*Bloomfield Avenue and continue along the edge of the*
*woods. Seventy-five yards past an intersection with Cargill*
*Lane, turn right into the woods and follow the footpath back*
*to the main trail.*

*After either crossing or bypassing the small stream as*
*described above, continue through a trail junction and then*
*uphill. Follow the wide path along the crest of the slope,*
*with Pennypack Creek (and a riverside trail) downhill to*
*the right. Eventually descend slowly along the flank of the*
*valley and pass below the Pennypack Environmental*
*Center. Continue as the path narrows and descends in*
*order to pass behind the Verree house and under the Verree*
*Road bridge.*

The Pennypack Environmental Center is administered by the
Fairmount Park Commission. The center is used to provide
environmental education for children. The Philadelphia school
system leases the Verree house. For information regarding the
workshops and nature programs run by the Pennypack Environmental Center, telephone 671-0440.

*After passing under Verree Road, bear left uphill. Turn*
*right into the woods on a dirt road. After crossing a stone*
*bridge, turn right through a picnic area, then veer half-left*
*on a wide path, which soon rejoins the river. Continue*
*downstream with the creek on the right. Eventually turn left*
*uphill away from the riverside trail. Climb through the*
*woods and into a clearing being used (as of 1982) to store*
*heaps of asphalt and telephone poles. Continue straight*
*over the top of the hill, then turn left at a T-intersection.*
*Follow the narrow path along the side of the slope, then*
*right downhill to an old road bordered by a stone wall*

above the river. Continue under a railroad bridge and along the creek to Krewstown Road.

At Krewstown Road turn left and follow the road uphill away from Pennypack Creek. At a railroad underpass cross the road and enter the woods on a wide bridle path above the river. After crossing a small bridge, fork right to continue downstream along the river's edge and under the Bustleton Avenue bridge. Eventually veer left away from the river and climb to Winchester Road. Follow the road several hundred yards back to your starting point.

**10**

# TYLER STATE PARK

*Walking and ski touring — 7.5 miles (12.1 kilometers). A
network of bicycle paths, horse trails, and tree-lined country
roads closed to motor vehicles. The route follows Neshaminy
Creek upstream to the Schofield Ford covered bridge. Return
through rolling farmland and woods. Open daily from 8:00 A.M.
until sunset. Dogs must be leashed. Telephone for information
about fishing, boating, ice skating, and canoe and bicycle
rental. Managed by the Bureau of State Parks (968-2021).*

---

THE SPECIAL CHARM of Tyler State Park is that much of
the land is farmed. About one quarter of the park's 1,700 acres is
planted in crops. Agricultural leases are awarded to the highest
bidders. The annual revenue (about $29,000 in 1982) is spent to
maintain state parks. Similarly, former farmhouses within the
park are occupied and maintained by tenants. Here, then, is an
opportunity to walk on country lanes through woods, meadows,
and cultivated fields.

If by now you have taken some of the walks outlined in this
book, you probably have noticed the striking variation in landforms presented by parks near Philadelphia. At Peace Valley
several watercourses that are frequently dry between rainfalls
weave through the woods at the bottom of a broad, shallow
valley. Wissahickon and Pennypack creeks have incised narrow, steep-sided valleys into the surrounding highlands. At
Morris Arboretum, Tyler State Park, and Ridley Creek State
Park, gently winding rivers flow through a rolling landscape, as
is typical of eastern Pennsylvania's Piedmont Plateau. Many
minor streams have cut tributary ravines into the high bluffs

*Thompson Dairy house (1775)*

bordering the Schuylkill River, which itself has carved a large valley through the region. The Delaware has worn an even wider course. At Tinicum and Rancocas parks, meandering tidal creeks flow across the flatlands. These varied streams and landscapes are good examples of the erosional cycle by which running water cuts into an elevated region and over the ages reduces it to a low plain.

Stream erosion is the dominant force at work shaping the world's landforms. Whenever any part of the earth's crust is raised above sea level, either by uplift of the land or withdrawal of the ocean as water is amassed in continental glaciers, the newly elevated surface is at once subject to the erosive power of water. Any downward-pitched trough, crevice, or fissure, even though at first shallow or insignificant, is self-aggrandizing, collecting to itself rainwater that falls on other areas. Initially such minor watercourses are dry between rains, but gradually they are deepened by erosion, and once they penetrate the water table, they are fed by a steady seepage of groundwater from the sides of the ravines.

As a stream extends itself by developing tributaries, its erosive power rapidly increases. The larger drainage area concentrates more water in the channel downstream, where stream energy is swelled both by the greater mass of moving water and by its greater depth, which results in proportionately less friction with the streambed. In consequence, the speed of the river increases and so does its ability to carry fine clay, silt, and sand in suspension and to push and roll pebbles and cobbles downstream.

Although at first erosion is fastest in the lower reaches of a river where volume is greater, the ocean constitutes a base level below which the stream cannot cut to any significant degree. As downward cutting approaches the base level, the site of the most rapid erosion slowly moves upstream.

Meanwhile, the lower river still possesses great energy, which is applied to eroding the bank wherever the stream is deflected by each slight turn. This tendency to carve wider and wider curves is present along the entire stream but is accentuated

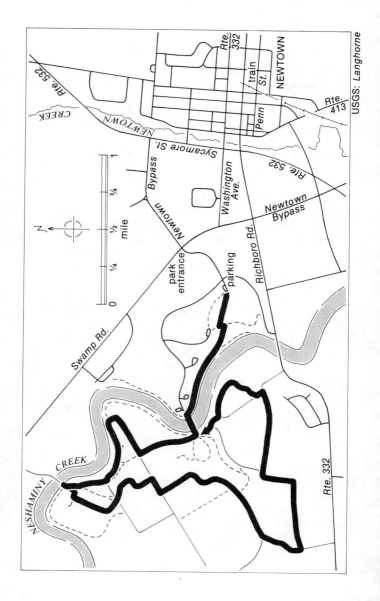

in the lower reaches, where downward cutting is no longer possible but where sideward cutting can continue as long as there is flow. Gradually, a meandering course develops as the river snakes back and forth, gnawing first at one side of the valley and then at the other. When sinuosity becomes so extreme that the river doubles back on itself, the current will intercept the channel farther downstream, cutting off the looping meander. Thus over the course of time the river migrates in an ever-changing, winding course over the bottomland, creating a valley much wider than it is deep and leaving behind abandoned channels here and there.

Another distinctive geologic feature develops at the mouth of the river where it empties into an ocean, estuary, or lake. As the current dissipates in the standing water, the capacity of the stream to carry material in suspension is reduced and then eliminated, so that the river's load of gravel, sand, and silt is dropped and forms a delta, as has occurred in Darby Creek at Tinicum. Because the current slows gradually, the deposition tends to be self-sorting, with larger particles dropped first. After the delta has extended itself a considerable distance in one direction, a flood may cut a new and shorter channel to open water, causing the former course to be abandoned, at least for a period. Deltas typically have several channels among which the stream shifts as deposition is concentrated first in one and then in another.

By focusing on the variables of stream gradient, valley depth, valley width, and number of meanders, you can determine a specific stage of erosional development for any stretch of river. In the earliest stage, the gradient of the streambed is relatively steep, and rapids are common. Because the dominant direction of cutting is downward, valleys and ravines are steep-sided and V-shaped, as at Wissahickon and Pennypack creeks. There are no flats in the valley bottoms. Valley depth relative to width is maximized. Such a stream is said to be in *youth*.

As the stream approaches base level, its gradient diminishes and downward cutting slows. The bends in the course of the stream become accentuated, and the width of the valley increases relative to its depth, as has occurred at Neshaminy Creek in Tyler State Park. At the point where sideward cutting becomes significant and a flat valley floor starts to develop, the stream is said to be in *maturity*.

Finally, when downward cutting has ceased and the stream is at base level, sideward cutting produces a nearly flat and featureless valley, much wider than it is deep, across which the river meanders from side to side. Such an erosional surface is called a *peneplain*. The gradient is low and the broad bottomland is marked only by the scars, swamps, and lakes left by former channels; perhaps a few rock hummocks and hills — more resistant to erosion than were their surroundings — are left as well. This stage of river development is *old age*.

Of course, the terms *maturity* and *old age* can best be applied only to sections of a stream because the uppermost valleys of a river and its tributaries always are in youth. Also, these terms do not describe the actual age of a stream but only its stage of development. Some streams develop faster than others, depending on the climate of the area, the resistance of the underlying rock to erosion, and other geologic events. For example, the Wissahickon Valley north of Philadelphia has a relatively gentle (i.e., old) profile compared to the youthful gorge downstream within the city. This anomaly is traceable to the fact that the downstream portion flows through an area of hard crystalline rock that is more resistant than the sandstone, shale, and limestone underlying the upstream section. Thus, the terrain along even a single river can reflect different stages of erosional development in no particular sequence, depending on the underlying materials.

The terms *youth, maturity,* or *old age* also can be used for an entire landscape or region to describe the extent to which it has been acted upon by stream erosion. As a region is dissected by the headward erosion of a stream system, more and more of the landscape is given over to a branching network of steep-sided valleys, ravines, and gullies, which gradually widen and develop flat valley bottoms. Focusing on the ratio among original upland, valley slope, and valley bottom, an area is said to be in

youth until about half of the original upland is consumed by valley slopes and the streams are just beginning to develop flats at the valley bottoms. As the percentage of upland diminishes further and the portion in the valley flats increases, the area is in maturity. At some point the upland lying between different tributaries or different stream systems is cut away until the divide changes from a wide, flat summit to a sharp-crested ridge that in turn is worn down to a low, rounded rise. Old age is said to start when more than half of the region is in valley bottom, and it continues as the whole region gradually is reduced to a peneplain. Thus, in general, youth is the time of dominant upland, maturity the time of dominant valley slope, and old age the time of dominant valley bottom.

*PUBLIC TRANSIT: Take the train from Reading Terminal to Foxchase, and from there take the High Speed Line (SEPTA HS-1) to Newtown. From the railroad station in Newtown, walk west on Penn Street toward the center of town. Turn right at an intersection with Court Street, then left at a T-intersection with Washington Avenue. Follow Washington Avenue across Newtown Creek and through a crossroads. Continue straight past Council Rock High School to a T-intersection with the Newtown Bypass. Turn right. At the next intersection turn left into Tyler State Park. Follow the entrance road downhill past the park office, through a crossroads, and straight into a parking lot for the Plantation Picnic Area. The walk from the train station totals 1.6 miles; most of it is very pleasant.*

*AUTOMOBILE: From Exit 28 off the Pennsylvania Turnpike, follow Route 1 (which is the eastward extension of Roosevelt Boulevard) northeast toward I-95. About 1.2 miles north of the Turnpike, avoid exiting on Route 1 to Morrisville; instead, continue on the expressway to I-95. Take I-95 north to the Newtown-Yardley exit (Route 332). Follow Route 332 west through Newtown, across Newtown Creek, and straight past Council Rock High School. At a*

*T-intersection with the Newtown Bypass, turn right. At the next intersection turn left into Tyler State Park. Follow the entrance road downhill past the park office, through a crossroads, and straight into a parking lot for the Plantation Picnic Area.*

*THE WALK:    Although the roads followed by this walk are closed to most automobile traffic, be alert for bicycles and occasional park vehicles.*

*From the lower end of the parking lot for the Plantation Picnic Area, follow an asphalt path (the Quarry Trail) past a baseball field on the left and a picnic area on the right. Continue downhill through the woods. Turn left at a pair of restrooms, then right onto Tyler Drive Trail. Join Neshaminy Creek on the left. Continue past several picnic and parking areas to a low concrete bridge below a dam.*

*After crossing the river, turn right upstream on a paved road. Pass a house on the right. At a T-intersection with Dairy Hill Trail, turn right. Follow the path downhill to the river's edge, then around to the left and back uphill. After passing by a meadow on the left (with a barn in the distance), fork right onto a dirt trail where the asphalt path veers left. Pass through a hedgerow and descend diagonally across two fields to a covered bridge.*

*From the covered bridge, return 100 yards by the way you came, but then continue straight uphill on a gravel road. Turn left at a group of farm buildings (now a youth hostel) and continue uphill on a paved road. Curve left at the top of the hill, then continue straight through a crossroads. Pass a barn on the left and a house on the right as the path winds downhill. Turn right at a T-intersection with Dairy Hill Trail, then left at the next intersection onto No. 1 Lane Trail. Again, pass between a barn and a house.*

*Continue on the asphalt road, eventually descending into the woods. Pass yet another barn and house. Fork left across a small stone bridge where College Park Trail veers right. After passing a house on the left, turn left onto Stable*

Mill Trail 30 yards beyond a small parking lot on the right. Continue straight past two more houses. Follow the path as it turns left, then right. Immediately after this second turn, continue straight on Stable Mill Trail instead of turning left on the Natural Area Trail.

Pass more farm buildings. Eventually, turn left onto Mill-Dairy Trail. Fork right immediately onto Woodfield Trail. At the next intersection, veer right in order to return along the river to the bridge below the dam. Cross the bridge and follow Tyler Drive Trail to the right downstream. Turn left onto Quarry Trail, then right by the restrooms to return to your starting point.

# 11

# RANCOCAS STATE PARK

*Walking and ski touring — 3 miles (4.8 kilometers). Dirt roads and footpaths lead through a flat landscape of woods and weedy fields. At times the trail overlooks Rancocas Creek. Open daily from 8:00 A.M. to 5:00 P.M. Managed by the New Jersey Department of Environmental Protection, Division of Parks and Forestry (609) 726-1191.*

*Adjacent to Rancocas State Park is the New Jersey Audubon Society's Rancocas Nature Center. Open daily except Monday from 9:00 A.M. to 5:00 P.M. Closed legal holidays. Dogs and picnicking are prohibited (609) 261-2495.*

---

ACCORDING TO THE STAGES of stream development discussed in the preceding chapter, the stretch of Rancocas Creek examined by this walk is old. The river meanders through a marshy flood plain. The stream has cut downward to sea level so that now the creek itself fluctuates with the tide. The river cannot cut deeper unless the ocean recedes or the land rises. Sideward cutting, however, continues. Appendages and ponds along the present course — bayous, in effect — mark former channels. Bordering the flood plain are small scarps carved by the river's sweeping curves. In some places the creek is gnawing at the foot of these bluffs, but in other areas the channel has shifted and is now located at the middle or opposite side of the flats.

The entire region through which the creek winds is a low, slightly undulating plain. In fact, all of southern New Jersey is part of the Atlantic Coastal Plain physiographic province that extends in a band of varying width from Massachusetts to

Florida. In the lower Delaware Valley, the Coastal Plain meets the Piedmont Plateau in a line stretching through Trenton, Bristol, Philadelphia, and Chester. Along this natural boundary, the hard crystalline rocks of the Wissahickon Formation (discussed in Chapter 5) dip southeastwardly under the thick beds of gravel, sand, silt, and clay that were deposited in the coastal region during periods when it was submerged beneath the sea. Not surprisingly, stream erosion has produced a much flatter, "older" landscape in the soft, unconsolidated materials of the Coastal Plain than it has in the harder — and in fact more ancient — Wissahickon rocks.

For the most part, however, the flat terrain of southern New Jersey is not the work of the present-day stream system; it is primarily the result of extensive stream erosion that occurred earlier, during periods between intervals of inundation by the sea. Also, sedimentation during the periods of submergence spread smoothing coats of sand and silt over the region. At present, southern New Jersey stands as a very slightly elevated plateau that is being dissected and reduced to a still lower plain by the streams we see today.

A history of extensive erosion is also indicated by the curious pattern in which soil materials occur throughout the region. For example, at Rancocas State Park a layer of light-colored, fine-grained quartz sand occurs 1 or 2 feet below the surface in an irregularly shaped belt stretching from northeast to southwest across the southern part of the state. On both sides of this formation are several other bands of different material, all trending in the same direction and each identifiable by a unique blend of sand, silt, clay, minerals, and marine fossils. The belts are thought to be sedimentary strata that, starting about 130 million years ago, were deposited as horizontal beds one on top of another during periods when the region was under water. The distinct composition of the layers may reflect the depth of each successive inundation, since sand tends to accumulate in shallow water, and clay and marine fossils in deeper areas. Although sea level fluctuated, subsidence of the entire region continued as the dominant movement. Gradually, however, the strata were

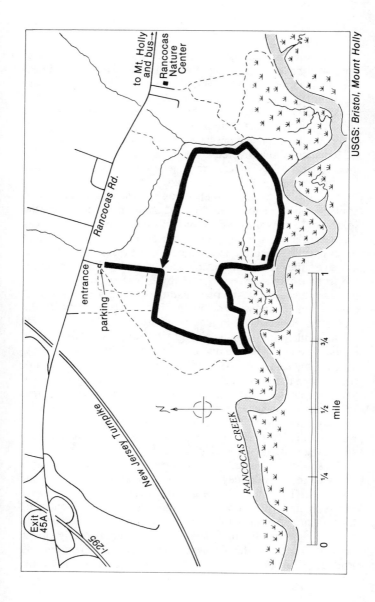

USGS: *Bristol, Mount Holly*

103

tilted toward the southeast. The seaward edge of the region sank, but the landward edge rose slightly. Erosion then reduced the elevated area to a horizontal plain, so that now the tilted sedimentary beds intersect the surface of the ground as a series of parallel bands. Recently (that is, starting about a million years ago), the strata were partially obscured at the surface by thin deposits of glacial outwash swept south from the continental ice sheets that covered Canada and the northern U.S. The most recent of these glaciers retreated from northern New Jersey less than twenty thousand years ago.

Records of soil material encountered when wells are drilled confirm the presence of different strata dipping slightly to the southeast. For example, one hole drilled just south of Rancocas State Park passed through a foot of topsoil and then penetrated the fine white sand typical of the area. At a depth of 120 feet, however, the driller encountered the bed of clay that is present at the surface about a mile to the northwest. At 187 feet down, the driller reached the distinctive mixture of clay, sand, and gravel that occurs at the surface in the immediate vicinity of the Delaware River, still farther northwest. Similarly, the fine white sand found near the surface in Rancocas State Park is encountered at 37 feet below sea level in wells at Mount Holly, 2 miles to the east of the park. Fifteen miles southeast of the park the same material is reached at 524 feet below sea level. At yet another 15 miles southeast, the same layer is found at 1,116 feet below sea level. Other wells show the same pattern. Considering any given layer, it is encountered at ever-greater depths in wells drilled farther and farther to the southeast of the area where the material is found at the surface.

An anomaly revealed by well records is that some of the strata are wedge-shaped: they get thicker as they dip toward the southeast. Thus the angle of dip is steeper for the older, lower layers. One explanation is that the regional movements that have occurred in the earth's crust resemble the half-stroke of a seesaw, with its fulcrum located near and roughly parallel to the present course of the Delaware River between Trenton and Philadelphia. The land to the northwest has risen while the coastal area to the southeast has sunk. This motion produces subsidence that is steadily deeper away from the fulcrum, thus allowing sediments to accumulate to a greater thickness toward the southeast.

*PUBLIC TRANSIT:    From the intersection of Broad and Cherry streets in downtown Philadelphia, take the Fort Dix–Mount Holly bus (Transport of New Jersey 71). Get off at the intersection of High Street and Garden Street in the center of Mount Holly. (On the west side of this intersection, Garden Street changes name to Rancocas Road.) You will know that your stop is coming when the bus turns left from Mill Street onto High Street. For information about the Mount Holly bus, call toll free in Pennsylvania (800) 526-4514; in New Jersey call (800) 772-2222.*

*From the bus stop walk 1.8 miles west on Rancocas Road to the New Jersey Audubon Society's Rancocas Nature Center on the left. Continue west 350 yards on Rancocas Road to a trail on the left marked by wooden posts and a single brick post. Follow the faint path away from the road along the left edge of an overgrown field. Bear right around the end of the field, then left into the woods. Cross a small stream and continue to a T-intersection at the edge of a weedy field. Turn right onto the trail circuit described below.*

*AUTOMOBILE:    Rancocas State Park is about 13 miles northeast of Camden and 2 miles west of Mount Holly. The park is easily reached from either I-295 or the New Jersey Turnpike.*

*From Philadelphia cross the Delaware River on the Walt Whitman Bridge or the Ben Franklin Bridge or the Tacony-Palmyra Bridge. From the Walt Whitman Bridge, bear left for I-295, then veer right for I-295 north to Trenton. From the Ben Franklin Bridge, follow Route 30, then Route 38 east more than 9 miles to I-295 north. From the Tacony-Palmyra Bridge, go 7 miles on Route 73 to I-295 north. In all three cases, follow I-295 north past the exit for Rancocas Woods,* then take the next exit for Mt. Holly and Willingboro. Veer right for Mt. Holly. Follow Rancocas Road 0.8 mile across the New Jersey Turnpike to the entrance for Rancocas State Park on the right. The park road is obscure, so be alert for the turn. The New Jersey Audubon Society's Rancocas Nature Center is 0.7 mile farther east on Rancocas Road.

Alternatively, from Philadelphia's northern suburbs, take the Pennsylvania Turnpike east across the Delaware River. Turn south toward Camden on the New Jersey Turnpike. Leave the New Jersey Turnpike at Exit 5 and follow the signs east to Mount Holly. In the center of Mount Holly, turn right from High Street onto Rancocas Road. Continue 2.5 miles to the park entrance on the left, passing (at 1.8 miles) the New Jersey Audubon Society's Rancocas Nature Center.

THE WALK:    From the small parking lot and gate of Rancocas State Park, follow the entrance road straight through the woods. Turn right at a crossroads at the edge of a clearing. Bear left at a T-intersection. With a weedy field on your right, follow the path to Rancocas Creek.

With your back to the water, turn right and follow the river's edge, at first on a grassy road and then on an obscure path along the high bank. Where the river turns right, bear left away from the creek. A hundred yards after emerging from the woods, turn right at a three-way intersection of dirt roads. Turn right again past a large cement-block structure. Follow the road as it dips down across a slough. Continue past a house to the river's edge at the end of the road.

Again, with your back to the river, turn right and follow the faint track along the crest of the embankment. At times the obscure path follows the edge of the bluff; at other times the path lies about 10 yards back from the edge. If the path appears to head down the slope, climb to the left and pick up the trail along the rim.

For one stretch the river lies out of sight to the right but then reappears. Where the river once again curves off to the right, follow the path away from the embankment. Continue

*through level woods to a T-intersection in front of a small
stream. (On the far side is the Audubon Sanctuary.)*

*Turn left in front of the stream. Continue 90 yards before
forking right onto a narrow path that soon follows a low
ridge on the right. Emerge at the corner of a weedy field.
Follow the path to the right along the edge of the field. Bear
left at the next corner and continue with woods on the right
and the overgrown field on the left. Pass a trail (which goes
to Rancocas Road) intersecting from the right. At the next
corner of the field, continue straight into the woods. Emerge
at the corner of another overgrown field. Continue straight
with the field on the left. Pass a trail intersecting from the
left. Turn right at a crossroads to return to the parking lot
and park entrance.*

## 12

# DELAWARE CANAL
## Yardley south to Morrisville
## Yardley north to Washington Crossing

*Walking and ski touring — up to 17 miles (27.4 kilometers) round trip. From Yardley hike south or north on the broad, level towpath of the Delaware Canal. Four miles south of Yardley is Morrisville. Four miles north of Yardley is the McConkey's Ferry section of Washington Crossing Historic Park, where the Continental Army crossed the Delaware River to attack Trenton. A visitor center and boathouse contain exhibits. Four and a half miles farther north along the canal is the Thompson's Mill section of the park. Hike as far as you want and return by the way you came. If you do not want to retrace your steps, a car shuttle is necessary.*

*The towpath is open daily from sunrise to sunset. Officially named Roosevelt State Park, the canal is managed by Pennsylvania's Bureau of State Parks (982-5560). Washington Crossing Historic Park is managed by the Pennsylvania Historical and Museum Commission in cooperation with the Washington Crossing Park Commission (493-4076). The visitor center is open from 9:00 A.M. to 5:00 P.M. on weekdays and Saturday; from noon to 5:00 P.M. on Sunday.*

T HE DELAWARE CANAL extends 60 miles along the Delaware Valley between Easton in the north and Bristol in the south, with Lumberville at the midpoint. Upstream from Morrisville (opposite Trenton) the waterway escapes the clutter of the metropolitan area. It stretches through woods and fields and

*Delaware Division of the Pennsylvania Canal*

passes old locks and spillways. Aqueducts carry the canal over streams that flow into the Delaware River. The canal goes by houses, inns, villages, and mills that grew up next to the waterway during the hundred years of its commercial operation — an era that ended in 1931. Nine years later, however, the canal was made a state park, and today the waterway is still largely intact. Hikers can follow the grassy towpath as far as they like, and refresh themselves at one of the inns in Washington Crossing, New Hope, Center Bridge, or Lumberville. Even nonwalkers can enjoy the waterway by taking a ride in a mule-drawn canal boat starting from New Hope (telephone 862-2842 for boat information). Also, canoes can be rented at various points along the canal (telephone 493-2366 in Washington Crossing, 297-8400 in Point Pleasant, or 749-2093 in Riegelsville).

Prior to completion of the canal in 1834, most products bound up or down the Delaware Valley were transported on the open river, despite its many rapids. As early as 1750 huge rafts of logs from New York State and northeastern Pennsylvania were floated to market in Philadelphia. One account from 1828 reports rafts 200 feet long by 60 feet wide. At times fifteen or twenty rafts could be seen at once. Sawmills sprang up at Trenton, Morrisville, Yardley, Taylorsville (now called Washington Crossing), Hendricks and Eagle islands, Lumberton, Lumberville, and other towns along the river. Spring flood was the best rafting season. In early May of 1875 one raftsman was told by the record keeper at the Lackawaxen Dam on the upper Delaware that 3,140 rafts had been counted so far that year. The dams had spillways at the center through which the rafts could pass downstream. Most raft traffic on the lower Delaware ceased by the end of the nineteenth century. In 1911 a sawmill operator at Lumberton recalled:

There were lively times during spring rafting freshets. I can see one float after another going down the river, the men looking like dressed-up ghosts as they silently swung their Brobdingnagian oars, and as if going to some mysterious country from which there was no returning.

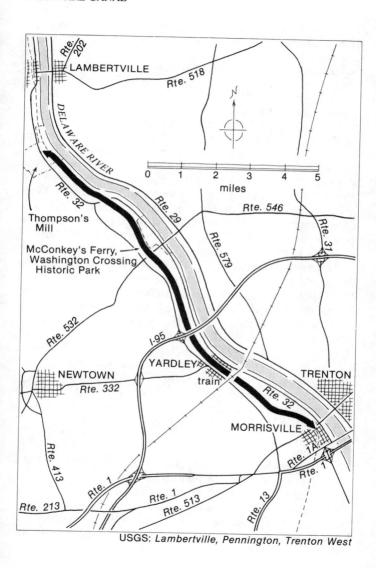

USGS: *Lambertville, Pennington, Trenton West*

Before the canal era, Durham boats were the chief means of transporting manufactured goods and agricultural products up and down the Delaware River. The first such boats are supposed to have been built by Robert Durham in the 1740s to transport iron produced at Durham Furnace, located 10 miles below Easton. The boats were 40 to 60 feet long, 8 feet wide, and pointed at each end like oversized canoes. They could carry up to 20 tons but even when loaded drew less than 3 feet. They were guided by long oars as they floated downstream with the current, but had to be poled laboriously back upstream by men pacing back and forth along the walking rails at the top of each gunwale. This was the type of boat used by George Washington and his troops to cross the Delaware on December 26, 1776, prior to their attack on the Hessian garrison at Trenton. A replica of a Durham boat and other early river craft can be seen in the boathouse at the McConkey's Ferry section of Washington Crossing Historic Park.

As early as December 1, 1776, Washington directed the seizure of all boats on the Delaware River for 70 miles above Philadelphia. He mentioned the Durham boats in particular. From New Brunswick, New Jersey, he wrote to inform Congress at Philadelphia that "we shall retreat to the West side of [the] Delaware."

> I have sent forward Colonel Humpton to collect proper boats and craft at the ferry for transporting our troops, and it will be of infinite importance to have *every other craft*, besides what he takes for the above purpose, secured on the west side of the Delaware, otherwise they may fall into the enemy's hands and facilitate their views.

The enemy's views were presumed to be the capture of Philadelphia. After evacuating Boston and withdrawing to Halifax in March of 1776, the British under General Sir William Howe had reappeared at New York, where on August 27 they badly defeated the Americans in the Battle of Long Island. On November 20 German mercenaries employed by England captured Fort Washington at the northern end of Manhattan Island.

About twenty-five hundred American soldiers were taken prisoner, a loss equal to the entire American force that later fought at Trenton.

By the end of November, Washington's army was retreating southwestward across New Jersey. Ten thousand British and German soldiers under Major General Cornwallis were in close pursuit. According to a report that Washington sent to the Continental Congress on November 23 from Newark, the American army numbered 5,410 troops, counting nearly two thousand men who a week later simply went home when their enlistments expired.

To weaken American resistance still further, General Howe issued a proclamation offering clemency to anyone who signed a statement promising that he would "remain in a peaceable Obedience to His Majesty." So many people appeared before British officials that the forms on which the loyalty oath was printed ran out. "The conduct of the Jerseys has been most infamous," Washington later wrote to his half-brother John Augustine.

> Instead of turning out to defend their country, and affording aid to our army, they are making their submissions as fast as they can. If they had given us any support, we might have made a stand at Hackensack and after that at Brunswick, but the few militia that were in arms, disbanded themselves . . . and left the poor remains of our army to make the best we could of it.

Cornwallis almost caught up with the Americans at Newark and then at New Brunswick, but Howe had instructed him to proceed no farther. Cornwallis sent an aide back to New York to seek permission to attack the American army before it crossed the Delaware. After a delay of five days, Howe joined Cornwallis with still more troops. Their combined force left New Brunswick on December 6. At Princeton the American rear guard slowed the British advance, while the rest of Washington's army crossed the Delaware at Trenton on December 7 and 8. The rear guard then raced to the river, where the last troops boarded the Durham boats and rowed to safety just as a Hessian brigade entered Trenton with brass band playing.

At first General Howe considered pushing on to Philadelphia. There were no bridges across the Delaware, so he sent Cornwallis up the river to Coryell's Ferry (present-day New Hope) to look for boats. None was found: all boats had been removed to the western bank. However, Washington had little reason to believe that this strategem would stop the British for long. They could bring their attack flatboats overland by wagon from New York or build new boats on the spot. At Trenton Howe had discovered 48,000 feet of lumber already cut into boards. Also, within a day's march of Trenton there were eight fords where the British could wade across the river. If the river froze, as often happened in January, the British could march across. "Upon the whole there can be no doubt that Philadelphia is their object, and that they will pass the Delaware as soon as possible," Washington wrote to Congress.

> Happy should I be if I could see the means of preventing them. At present I confess I do not. All military writers agree, that it is a work of great difficulty, nay impracticable, where there is any extent of coast to guard. This is the case with us and we have to do it with a force small and inconsiderable and much inferior to that of the enemy . . . . Our little handful daily decreasing by sickness and other causes: and without aid, without considerable succours and exertions on the part of the people, what can we reasonably look for or expect, but an event that will be severely felt by the common Cause and that will wound the heart of every virtuous American — the loss of Philadelphia?

In expecting the British to press their advantage, Washington was reasonable, and he was realistic — but he was wrong. He had not, of course, reckoned on the British commander's characteristic lack of energy and initiative. On December 12 the winter's first snow began (until then the weather had been extraordinarily mild), and on the next day General Howe decided to call off the campaign for that year. New Jersey appeared to have been pacified by his program of pardon and reconciliation. After the military reverses suffered by the Americans during the summer and fall, enthusiasm for the Revolution was declining. Also, Howe had intercepted one of Washington's letters and knew that the enlistment of more than half of Washington's remaining force expired on January 1. Howe evidently believed that the rebel army — poorly clothed, ill-equipped, and demoralized — would by spring dissolve of its own accord. So he distributed his troops in a chain of garrisons stretching from Burlington to Hackensack and returned to New York, where he had an attractive mistress. Cornwallis prepared to sail for England, where his wife was ill. He would come back in the spring "if there is another campaign, which we doubt."

Despite the setbacks of the last half-year — or perhaps because of them — Washington immediately contemplated a counterthrust. He was fully aware that decisive and victorious action was essential if new recruits were to be raised and if the public, the state legislatures, and the various state militia were to support the Revolution. As early as December 13 Washington wrote to Governor Jonathan Trumbull in Connecticut that he was hoping "to attempt a stroke upon the Forces of the Enemy, who lay a good deal scattered and to all appearances in a state of security." The three regiments of Hessian mercenaries garrisoned for the winter at Trenton were a conspicuous target. German outposts around the town were attacked daily by American patrols sent across the river. The Hessians were intimidated into staying within the immediate vicinity of the village, except when they went out in large parties, hauling cannons with them. Yet the Hessian commander, Colonel Rall, was so contemptuous of the Americans' military ability that he failed to fortify the town. "Let them come!" he told one of his officers. "We want no trenches! We'll go after them with the bayonet!"

On December 22 John Honeyman, a butcher and cattle dealer who supplied the Hessians with meat, was captured by an American patrol outside of Trenton. He was taken to Washington, who interrogated him personally and in private. Washington, in fact, had met Honeyman at Hackensack in November, and had hired him as his personal spy, an arrangement that was known to no one else. Honeyman told Washington everything he knew about the German garrison at Trenton, where he had spent the preceding week. At the conclusion of the interview, Washington ordered Honeyman put under arrest, but the prisoner "escaped" that night. By December 24 Honeyman found his way back to Trenton, where he reported his adventure to Colonel Rall. The American army, Honeyman said, was incapable of a large action. It lacked clothes, shoes, food, and equipment necessary for a march. By British and German standards, this was largely true. The comforting news confirmed Rall's belief that the Americans could do nothing to harm him. Only the day before he had dismissed as "women's talk" the report by a loyalist that the Americans were readying themselves for a march of several days.

On December 23 Washington had in fact issued orders that the troops were to prepare a supply of cold food for three days. After his conversation with Honeyman, he wrote to Colonel Joseph Reed at Bristol that "Christmas Day at night, one hour before the day, is the time fixed upon for our attempt on Trenton. For Heaven's sake, keep this to yourself, as the discovery of it may prove fatal to us; our numbers, sorry I am to say, being less than I had any conception of; but necessity, dire necessity will, nay must, justify my attack."

The battle plan called for Colonel John Cadwalader to cross the Delaware River at Bristol with about a thousand newly raised Pennsylvania militia and five hundred regular troops. They were to engage the enemy garrison at Bordentown to prevent help being sent to Trenton. A mile below Trenton, Brigadier General James Ewing was to cross the Delaware with seven hundred Pennsylvanians to block the Hessians if they tried to retreat southward across Assunpink Creek, a tributary of the Delaware River. Washington himself, with twenty-four hundred regulars, was to cross at McConkey's Ferry, 9 miles above Trenton, then march south to attack the town.

Early on Christmas afternoon Washington's troops assembled

behind a ridge west of the ferry landing. As soon as darkness fell, the Durham boats, which had been hidden behind Malta Island farther upstream, were brought down to the crossing point. Late in the day Washington received a letter from Reed saying that General Israel Putnam, the hero of Bunker Hill, refused to bring his troops out from Philadelphia to join the foray into New Jersey because he was afraid loyalists would seize the city if he left. Next Cadwalader reported that his militiamen could not be relied on to fight. Washington replied, "Notwithstanding the discouraging accounts I have received from Colonel Reed of what might be expected from the operations below, I am determined, as the night is favorable, to cross the river and make the attack upon Trenton in the morning. If you can do nothing real at least create as great a diversion as possible."

An American officer at McConkey's Ferry wrote in his diary on December 25:

6:00 p.m. The regiments have had their evening parade but instead of returning to their quarters are marching toward the ferry. It is fearfully cold and raw and a snow storm is setting in. The wind is northeast and beats in the faces of the men. It will be a terrible night for the men who have no shoes. Some of them have tied old rags around their feet. Others are barefoot, but I have never heard a man complain. They are ready to suffer any hardship and die rather than give up their liberty.

Washington was among the first to cross the river. The big boats were rowed by men from Colonel John Glover's regiment of sailors from Marblehead, Massachusetts. Chunks of sheet ice on the river hit the boats and pushed them downstream. Loading eighteen cannons and their draft horses took longer than expected. It was three o'clock in the morning before the entire force was brought across. The advance toward Trenton had been planned to begin at midnight but did not get under way until four o'clock, with only three hours of darkness left.

At Trenton, Colonal Rall had continued to ignore one warning after another. On Christmas he received a letter from the British commander in New Jersey stating that the Americans might attack. That evening one of his sentries on the north side of Trenton was killed by a small Continental force that, without orders from Washington, had crossed the river and fired on a German outpost. Rall assembled his soldiers, forced the raiders to retreat, and then dismissed the incident. That evening, while Rall was drinking and playing cards, Moses Doane, an American loyalist and leader of a band of marauders who preyed on supporters of the Revolution, tried to see the German commander. Doane was denied admittance, but he sent in a note, which Rall put in his pocket unread.

Sleet fell as the Americans advanced toward Trenton in two columns by separate roads. At one point Washington received a message from one of his generals: "Muskets wet and can't be fired." Washington replied, "Tell your General to use the bayonet. The town must be taken." Yet many troops were without bayonets, and few had been trained in their use. The plan appeared to be going awry in other ways also. As dawn came, Washington's troops met the soldiers who had skirmished with the Germans the prior evening. Washington was furious, telling their officer, "You, sir, may have ruined all my plans by having put them on their guard." Also, unknown to Washington, Cadwalader had taken his troops across the river and then back again when their artillery could not be unloaded because of ice along the New Jersey shore. General Ewing and his militia opposite Trenton did not event attempt the crossing.

Sunrise came at seven-twenty in the morning but it was not until eight o'clock that the attack began. The Americans advanced at a trot from north and east toward the outskirts of the small town of about a hundred and thirty houses. The German guards fell back, shouting the alarm to turn out. The Americans were able to set up their artillery at the ends of the principal streets and to seize many of the houses before the three German regiments were fully formed. After a brief artillery duel, an American charge captured the only two cannons the mercenaries brought into play. Firing from doorways and windows and

*Soldier's grave at Washington Crossing Historic Park*

To y.ᵉ Memory of Cap.ᵗ
James Moore of y.ᵉ new
York Artillery S.ᵒ Son
of Benj.ⁿ & Cornelia
Moore of new York he
died Decm. y.ᵉ 25.ᵗʰ AD
1776 Ag.ᵈ 24 Years &
Eight Mon.ˢ

raking the streets with grapeshot, the Continental troops pushed the Germans back. Described by some historians as a "brawl" or a "kind of large-scale riot," the battle continued in the sleet for about an hour before one of the German regiments broke and fled to the southwest across a bridge over Assunpink Creek. This route was soon blocked by the Americans. With his two remaining regiments, Colonel Rall tried to force an escape to the north but was stopped by cannon fire. He ordered his men to fall back and, a moment later, toppled from his horse, mortally wounded. Soon afterward the Germans surrendered. The note that Rall had failed to read the night before was found in his pocket: "Washington is coming on you down the river, he will be here afore long. Doan."

The American victory was unqualified. Although 300 to 400 Germans escaped, 868 were captured and 106 were killed or wounded. Four Americans were wounded, and several others died — not from bullets but from the cold. Some of the Americans broke into the Germans' supply of rum, but Washington ordered forty hogsheads of liquor to be spilled into the street. The rest of the day was spent ferrying the exhausted army and their prisoners back across the Delaware River. In the process several more Americans collapsed and died of exposure.

The victory at Trenton galvanized the moribund patriot cause. Cadwalader, reinforced by militia from Philadelphia and believing that Washington was still at Trenton, finally managed to cross the river on December 27. In New Jersey the militia started to turn out. The Hessians abandoned Burlington and Bordentown. After learning that Washington was back in Pennsylvania, Cadwalader urged the Commander in Chief to join him to "keep up the panic." On December 30 Washington again brought his army across to Trenton. On the same day about half of the men whose enlistments expired on January 1 agreed, for a bounty of ten dollars, to serve six weeks more.

After joining forces with Cadwalader, Washington found himself at the head of an army of about five thousand men, more than half of whom were Pennsylvania militia, most without battle experience. By evening of January 2 this army was confronted at Trenton by a force of seven thousand German and British regulars who had marched south from Princeton. During the night, with campfires left burning and rags tied to the wheels of their artillery to muffle their movement, the Americans sneaked away. Circling north, they defeated an enemy garrison of twelve hundred at Princeton the next day. The British at Trenton rushed north again, but Washington moved to a strong position at Morristown, where the American army spent the winter. Shaken, the British withdrew from almost all of New Jersey. A Virginia loyalist, after passing through the state, wrote in his diary:

> The minds of the people are much altered. A few days ago they had given up their cause for lost. Their late successes have turned the scale and now they are all liberty mad again. Their recruiting parties could not get a man, . . . now men are coming in by companies . . . . They have recovered their panic and it will not be an easy mattter to throw them into that confusion again.

Lord George Germain, the British secretary of state for the Colonies, put it more succinctly: "All our hopes were blasted by the unhappy affair at Trenton."

*PUBLIC TRANSIT: From Reading Terminal take the train to Yardley. From the station in Yardley, walk north one block on Main Street, then turn right onto Letchworth Avenue. Cross the canal and descend to the towpath.*

*AUTOMOBILE: From Exit 28 off the Pennsylvania Turnpike, follow Route 1 (which is the eastward extension of Roosevelt Boulevard) northeast toward I-95. About 1.2 miles north of the Turnpike, avoid exiting on Route 1 to Morrisville; instead, continue on the expressway to I-95. Take I-95 north to the Newtown-Yardley exit (Route 332). Follow Route 332 east into Yardley. The canal and towpath can be reached by taking Afton Avenue or College Avenue or Letchworth Avenue east from Main Street.*

Because the most interesting part of this walk is between the southern section (McConkey's Ferry) and the northern section (Thompson's Mill) of Washington Crossing Historic Park, you may prefer to start not at Yardley but farther north at McConkey's Ferry, where Route 532 crosses the canal and the Delaware River. From Yardley drive north 4 miles along the Delaware River on Route 32. The park's visitor center is near the river on Route 32 just north of the intersection with Route 532. The canal and towpath pass under Route 532 about ½ mile west of the Delaware River.

THE WALK:   To reach Morrisville from Yardley, walk south 4 miles along an attractive section of the canal. Return the way you came.

The McConkey's Ferry section of Washington Crossing Historic Park is 4 miles north from Yardley. With the canal on the left, follow the towpath. At Route 532 in Washington Crossing (also called Taylorsville), the park visitor center and boathouse can be reached by following Route 532 east 0.4 mile, then Route 32 north a few hundred yards.

From the bridge where the canal passes under Route 532 in Washington Crossing, the Thompson's Mill section of the park is 4.5 miles farther north. With the canal on the left, follow the towpath, at one point crossing Route 32. Immediately north of the Route 32 bridge, the canal itself is carried by an aqueduct over Jericho Creek. Eventually pass a wide lawn and memorial to the soldiers of the Continental Army who died of sickness and exposure prior to the Battle of Trenton. Behind the memorial next to the river are a few graves. Turn left across the next bridge over the canal. Follow the paved path uphill to the Thompson-Neely House. Cross Route 32 to Thompson's Mill and the wildflower preserve.

If you have not arranged a car shuttle, return by the way you came.

The oldest part of the Thompson-Neely House was built in 1702 by John Pidock, who also established the gristmill across the road. During the Revolutionary War the house was occupied by two families, the Thompsons and the Neelys. In December 1776, however, their home was used as the headquarters of Major General William Alexander, who directed the American defenses along the river. Although a patriot, Alexander was also called Lord Stirling because of his claim to the earldom of Stirling in Scotland. An Edinburgh jury had accepted his claim but the House of Lords rejected it. Among the other officers quartered at the Thompson-Neely House was Lieutenant James Monroe, later president. It is said that Washington met here with his officers in the kitchen to plan the attack on Trenton.

**13**

# DELAWARE CANAL
## New Hope to Lumberville

*Walking and ski touring — up to 13 miles (20.9 kilometers)
round trip. From New Hope north to Lumberville along the
Delaware Canal. For long stretches the canal and towpath
border the Delaware River. Endurance specialists can hike 35
miles to Easton. Go as far as you want and return the way you
came. If you do not want to retrace your steps, a car shuttle is
necessary.*

*The towpath is open daily from sunrise to sunset. Officially
named Roosevelt State Park, the canal is managed by the
Bureau of State Parks (982-5560).*

---

**D**URING THE PERIOD of its commercial operation, the Delaware Canal was called the Delaware Division of the Pennsylvania Canal. The Pennsylvania Canal was a system of interconnected, state-financed waterways linked with other canals built as private ventures. The state canals were managed by the Pennsylvania Canal Commission, which had been formed in 1822 to develop a canal network to compete with the Erie Canal, then under construction and designed to join the Great Lakes and the Hudson River. Pennsylvanians justifiably feared that the Erie project would divert commerce from their state and from Philadelphia, which at that time was the nation's financial center. After the Erie Canal was opened in 1825, a wave of frenzied canal building swept the eastern states. Within two decades approximately 4,000 miles of canals were built. By the mid-1830s Pennsylvania's canal projects entailed state obligations

exceeding three times the commonwealth's annual revenue. Pennsylvania alone built more than 1,200 miles of canal, of which the 60 miles of the Delaware Division were just a small part.

The main purpose of the Delaware Canal was to transport coal. In 1791 anthracite was found near the town of Mauch Chunk (Jim Thorpe) in the Lehigh Valley. At first, little came of this discovery. Transporting coal in wagons down from the mountains to the Lehigh River was difficult and costly, and the river was too rocky and shallow to ensure safe shipment of coal to market. For that matter, there *was* no market. Heating stoves of the day were designed to burn wood. The iron industry still used charcoal for smelting ore. Steam engines were in their infancy, particularly in this country, where water power was abundant.

Gradually, however, a demand for coal was created. Josiah White, who with his associates leased the Mauch Chunk coal fields in 1818, promoted the development of new coal-burning stoves. The first models appeared in 1820 and caught on quickly. In 1822 the Lehigh Coal and Navigation Company was chartered, with White at the helm. Under his direction the coal company constructed the first coal railroad in the country. Powered by gravity, the loaded cars rolled downhill for 9 miles from the mines to the Lehigh River; mules pulled the empty cars back uphill. The coal company also made the Lehigh River navigable, after a fashion. Boulders were cleared from the channel. Dams with openings at their centers turned the river into a series of long pools and short chutes through which so-called arks were floated downstream. By 1823 arks loaded with coal were sent regularly from Mauch Chunk to Philadelphia.

The arks were made of dressed timbers strapped together with iron bands. These clumsy craft were strung together in tandem, sometimes reaching an overall length of 180 feet. Propelled by the current and guided by long oars, they were floated down the Lehigh River to its confluence with the Delaware River at Easton, and then on to Philadelphia. The arks were so cumber-

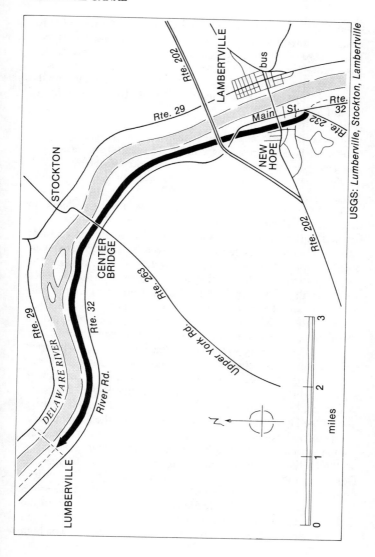

some that they could not be brought back upstream, so after the coal was unloaded, they were dismantled and sold for timber. There were other disadvantages. Coal bound for other cities, principally New York, had to be transferred to coastal vessels for the second half of the journey. Also, navigation through the dam openings was hazardous. On June 8, 1830, *The Whig* of Easton reported:

> An ark belonging to the Lehigh Coal and Navigation Company sunk on the 6th instant, in passing the sluice of the dam at this place. The men hung onto the oars, and were taken off by a skiff sent from shore to their rescue. The coal (about 140 tons) was lost.

As the commerce in coal increased, so did the demand for dependable, inexpensive water transportation. With the newly opened Erie Canal as an example (it reduced freight costs by half), construction began on the privately financed Delaware and Hudson Canal in 1825. This waterway was designed to carry coal from northeastern Pennsylvania to the Hudson River and New York. Also in 1825 the Morris Canal was started from the Delaware River opposite Easton to Jersey City and New York. Another private venture, the Morris Canal featured inclined railways to carry the canal boats between different sections of the waterway. It too was intended primarily to transport coal. In 1827 the Lehigh Coal and Navigation Company began construction of the Lehigh Canal. A series of short canals with locks was built around the dams on the Lehigh River. That same year the Commonwealth of Pennsylvania undertook construction of the Delaware Canal. It was linked with the Lehigh Canal at Easton and extended south to tidewater at Bristol, where boats could continue to Philadelphia under tow by sidewheel steamers on the Delaware River. Finally, in 1830 the privately financed Delaware and Raritan Canal was started. It connected Bordentown below Trenton on the Delaware River with the Raritan River and New York. A feeder canal carried water from the Delaware River above New Hope to the main Delaware and Raritan Canal at Trenton. Later, outlet locks were added on both sides of the Delaware River at New Hope. Canal boats were transferred from the Delaware Canal, across the river, to the Delaware and Raritan system. This crossing became one of the main routes for transporting Lehigh coal to New York.

The Lehigh Canal was completed in 1829, but the Delaware Division did not open until three years later. The canal leaked because its raised banks, which are essentially dikes, were made of sandy soil. The water level was insufficient, and the first boats could be only partially loaded. Large sections of the waterway were reworked under the direction of Josiah White, and a water wheel was constructed at New Hope to pump additional water into the canal from the Delaware River. By 1834, when the canal was declared satisfactory for boats loaded up to 70 tons, the cost of the project had exceeded twice the original estimate.

A report of the Canal Commissioners in 1830 summarizes the main features of the Delaware Canal:

> On this division the width of the canal at bottom is 25 feet, at top water line 40 feet, and its depth of water, 5 feet. In its course there are 23 lift locks, ranging from 6 to 10 feet lift, also 2 outlet and 2 guard locks. The canal and locks are arranged for boats of 67 tons burden. Eighteen lock keepers are necessary in this division.

The lift locks — 11 feet wide and 95 feet long, with mitered gates at each end — compensated for an overall drop in the Delaware River of 165 feet between Easton and Bristol. At any given time, one pair of gates for each lock was shut. Boats that were headed south toward Bristol entered the locks when the downstream gates were closed and the upstream gates open. The upstream gates were then closed behind the boat. Sluices in the downstream gates were opened to drain the water in the lock to the level of the canal below. Then the downstream gates were opened and the boat was towed out.

For boats headed upstream the procedure was reversed. After a boat had entered the lock and the downstream gates had been closed behind it, water was let into the lock through sluices in the upstream gates. When the level had risen to the same height as above the lock, the upstream gates were opened. The boat crews usually helped the lock keepers with the tasks of opening and closing the gates and sluices in order to pass through the lock as quickly as possible. In some places, such as New Hope, several locks in close succession were managed by a single keeper.

In addition to the locks there were stop gates, waste weirs, and overflow sluices at various points along the canal. The stop gates could be closed to seal off sections of the canal in case of flood or breaches in the canal bank. Waste weirs allowed the canal to be drained, and overflow sluices diverted excess water into the Delaware River.

One of the great advantages of the canal system was that it allowed coal to be shipped from mine to market without repeated unloading and reloading. The canal boats had to be able to fit through all segments of the canal network, however, and so a standard canal boat — called the *hinge boat, section boat,* or *snapper* — evolved.

The standard hinge boat was 10½ feet wide to fit the narrow locks of the Delaware Division. It was 87½ feet long, but the bow and stern halves — each of which floated independently of the other — could be separated. The two sections were held together by metal fittings and pins when the boat was under tow. The separate sections of the hinge boat could be handled more easily than could stiff (i.e., conventional) boats on the inclined railway of the Morris Canal. When coal was loaded and unloaded, the hinge boats could adjust better to the unequal weight in the forward and aft sections. Also, by unfastening and turning each half separately, a hinge boat could be turned around more easily than a stiff boat.

The sides of a hinge boat were straight and the bottom flat to maximize capacity in the shallow canal and to rest easily on the flatbed cradles of the Morris Canal railway. The deck also was nearly flat and without superstructure so that the boat could fit under bridges, even when the hold was empty and the boat was floating high. The sides tapered abruptly in front to form a

V-shaped prow with a vertical profile. A small cabin in the squared-off stern provided sleeping quarters for the crew — a captain or helmsman, a bow man, and a mule driver to lead the team along the towpath. Toward the end of the canal era, boats were operated without bow men, whose principal function was to help the boats through locks, in order to reduce costs.

Most of the boats that plied the Delaware Canal were owned by the Lehigh Coal and Navigation Company. The captains were paid for each trip completed from the coal mines to market and back. Some captains owned their own boats or worked for independent freight companies. The captains hired their crews — often members of their families — and supplied their own mule teams.

The canal operated for eight or nine months each year from April through November or December. In winter, when the waterway was closed because of ice, the canal was drained so that repairs could be made to the embankment and to the locks, aqueducts, and other equipment. Before dredges came into use, accumulations of silt were removed with shovels and wheelbarrows. Up and down the waterway empty boats were allowed to sit on the bottom of the canal near the homes of the boat captains. Occasionally during hard times a boatman and his family might spend the winter in one of the coal company's boats, using not only the cabin in the stern but also the hold for living quarters.

As spring approached the boatmen refurbished their equipment. The mules were reshod, the harnesses repaired and rubbed with oil, and the cabins cleaned and repainted. If the captain owned his boat, he might repaint the entire hull. New tow lines and snubbing ropes were purchased. After a warning from the section superintendent, water was let back into the canal by closing the waste weirs and opening all the locks, including those joining with the Lehigh River.

Once the boats started moving in the spring, they hardly stopped until fall. The locks were operated between 4:00 A.M. and 10:00 P.M. In the dark the boats were guided by "night hawkers," which were oil lamps with large reflectors. Men and mules ate on the move. Quick round trips were achieved primarily by working long hours rather than by moving faster. A team of three mules could haul a loaded boat at a steady pace of about 2 miles per hour, day after day, wearing out six pairs of shoes per season. Horses, though faster, quickly broke down.

The locks were major bottlenecks, and sometimes the boats backed up. Markers were set at equal distances above and below each lock. When two boats approached a lock from the same or opposite directions, the one that passed the marker first was supposed to be given priority through the lock. At night the boats tied up along the bank and the mules were put into one of many stables that catered to canal traffic. Often the boats started before 4:00 A.M. in order to arrive at the next lock by the time it opened.

During the middle decades of the nineteenth century, coal traffic on the Delaware Canal steadily increased. In 1833 about 92,000 tons were hauled. By 1840 the annual total was 171,000 tons, and by mid-century 581,000 tons. The peak year was 1866, when 792,397 tons of coal were transported down the canal. Over a thousand coal boats may have been in use on the Delaware Division that year, each making an average of twenty-three trips of seven to eight days' duration from Mauch Chunk to Bristol and back.

The canal was used to transport other commodities as well, including limestone, iron and iron ore, cement, plaster, grain, flour, hay, and whiskey. In 1867 a total of 901,000 tons was carried on the Delaware Division, of which 137,000 tons were not coal. Given the dominance of the coal traffic, it is not surprising that about 95 percent of the load carried by the canal was descending traffic. Most of the boats came back empty, although large quantities of guano, brick, milled lumber, salt, and general merchandise were brought up the canal.

During its peak years the Delaware Division was managed not by the Commonwealth of Pennsylvania but by the Lehigh Coal and Navigation Company. Anticipating a decline in traffic because of the advent of railroads, the state sold the canal in 1858 to the Sunbury and Erie Railroad Company, from which the waterway immediately was purchased by a newly organized subsidiary of the coal company. During the period of its control, the coal company maintained the canal in excellent condition and even made many improvements, despite the decline in traffic that set in after the Civil War. By 1880 the canal was carrying less than half the coal it had transported fifteen years earlier. In 1904, after a year of destructive floods, only 75,000 tons of coal were shipped down the canal. Repairs were made and in 1911 the waterway transported 321,000 tons, still hauled by mule-drawn canal boats. During the next two decades, the annual traffic gradually declined as the coal company moved more and more of its output by railroad. On the last day of 1917 the canal superintendent, I. M. Church, wrote in his diary:

> This was one hell of a year — labor scarce, high water, no boatmen, food high, cost sheet going wrong way and everybody with chips on their shoulders. Nothing but fight, fight. Hell has no terror — can't be anything worse then trying to run a damn old ditch like this.

In 1931, with only twenty boats left in operation, the Delaware Canal closed. That same year the Lehigh Coal and Navigation Company gave most of the canal to the Commonwealth of Pennsylvania. Governor Gifford Pinchot, who had been chief of the U.S. Forest Service under President Theodore Roosevelt, named the facility Roosevelt State Park. For a period the waterway reverted to the coal company when the gift was declared invalid due to legal irregularities, but in 1940, pursuant to a special act authorizing the state to acquire the canal by donation, ownership of the entire waterway was transferred to the commonwealth. Since then most of the canal has been maintained in good condition for recreation, although funds are chronically in short supply.

*PUBLIC TRANSIT:   From Olney station near the northern end of the Broad Street subway line, take SEPTA bus 55 to Doylestown. Get off at the end of the line at Cross Keys Terminal. From there take the West Hunterdon Transit Com-*

*pany's bus to Lambertville in New Jersey. For information about the bus to Lambertville, call (201) 782-6313 or (201) 996-2678.*

*From the bus stop in Lambertville, follow Bridge Street ½ mile west across the Delaware River to New Hope. Continue through an intersection with Main Street to a small bridge over the canal. Descend to the right to reach the towpath.*

*AUTOMOBILE: From Exit 28 off the Pennsylvania Turnpike, follow Route 1 (which is the eastward extension of Roosevelt Boulevard) northeast toward I-95. About 1.2 miles north of the Turnpike, avoid exiting on Route 1 to Morrisville; instead, continue on the expressway to I-95. Take I-95 north past the Newtown-Yardley exit (Route 332). Leave I-95 at the next interchange and follow Upper River Road and then Route 32 north 9 miles to New Hope.*

*Alternatively, from Exit 27 off the Pennsylvania Turnpike, follow Easton Road (Route 611) north to Doylestown, and from there take Route 202 east to New Hope.*

*Parking is difficult in New Hope; spaces are easier to find on the edge of town. Join the towpath where the canal passes under Bridge Street one block west of Main Street.*

New Hope is named for the flour, linseed oil, and lumber mills of Benjamin Parry. In 1790 the mills were destroyed by fire, but Parry rebuilt, calling them the New Hope Mills. The Parry gristmill is now the Bucks County Playhouse. Opposite the playhouse is the remodeled stone Parry barn. Across Main Street at the corner with Ferry Street are the Parry Mansion, managed by the New Hope Historical Society, and the Logan Inn, successor to various hostelries dating back to the early eighteenth century. Farther toward the river on Ferry Street is a small stone building that was once the New Hope Library and before that the toll house for Coryell's Ferry (as New Hope was called during the Revolution).

Immediately south of the Ferry Street bridge over the canal, a small aqueduct carries the canal across Ingham Creek. Water power from the creek made New Hope one of Bucks County's leading industrial towns in the early nineteenth century.

The remains of four double locks, with a combined drop of 30 feet, are located a few hundred yards farther south along the canal. The lock keeper's house and toll collector's office are now private studios and homes. Part of the lock system is on the far side of Main Street, as are the remains of the outlet to the Delaware River, where boats were ferried across to an arm of the Delaware and Raritan Canal. The mules were taken around by way of the bridge to Lambertville.

*THE WALK:   After inspecting the canal and locks at the southern end of New Hope, follow the towpath north out of town. Continue with the canal on the left. The canal passes under many small bridges and several large ones, including the Route 202 highway bridge and the Route 263 bridge, both over the Delaware River. Pass Hendrick Island. Continue for a total of 6 miles to the suspension bridge, specialty shops, and Black Bass Hotel, restaurant, and bar in Lumberville. To reach the village continue 175 yards under the suspension bridge, then turn left across a small bridge below Lock No. 12.*

*If you have not arranged a car shuttle, return the way you came.*

As its name implies, Lumberville started as a lumber center and sawmill to which logs, gathered into large rafts, were floated down the Delaware River. The Black Bass Hotel has existed here since 1745. The footbridge, built in 1949 to replace a toll bridge, crosses to the Bull's Island section of the Delaware and Raritan Canal State Park in New Jersey. The bridge-tender's house stands at the Pennsylvania end of the bridge.

# 14

# PEACE VALLEY NATURE CENTER

*Walking and ski touring — 1 or more miles (1.6 or more kilometers). A network of trails through fields and woods at the eastern end of Lake Galena. The Nature Center is a 300-acre wildlife refuge within 1,500-acre Peace Valley Park. Good birding. Open daily from 8:00 A.M. until sunset. Dogs must be leashed. Picnicking is prohibited. Managed by the Bucks County Department of Parks and Recreation (757-0571).*

---

**B**ECAUSE OF THE VARIETY of its habitats — weedy fields, thickets, deciduous woods, sluggish streams, a lake, swampy shallows, and mud flats — the Peace Valley Nature Center north of Doylestown is among the better places near Philadelphia to see a wide assortment of birds. More than 240 species of waterfowl, land birds, and migrating shore birds have been recorded — or about 75 percent of all species that occur regularly in the Delaware Valley region.

Even for fledgling birders, identifying the many species at Peace Valley is easier than might at first be thought. Shape, size, plumage, and other physical characteristics are distinguishing field marks; other considerations such as range, season, habitat, song, and behavior are just as useful. Together, these factors are the key to identifying birds.

Range is of primary importance for the simple reason that many birds are not found throughout North America or even Pennsylvania, but only in certain regions such as the Atlantic and Gulf coasts. For example, Cedar Waxwings and Bohemian Waxwings closely resemble each other, but the latter is not seen in Pennsylvania. The better field guides provide maps of bird

*Yarrow,* Achillea millefolium

ranges based on years of reported sightings and bird counts. Of course, bird ranges are not static. Some pioneering species, such as the Glossy Ibis and House Finch, have extended their ranges during recent decades, while other birds, such as the Ivory-billed Woodpecker, have perhaps even died out.

Season is related to range, inasmuch as migratory birds are found in different parts of their ranges during different times of year. The spotted-breasted thrushes, for instance, are sometimes difficult to distinguish from each other, but usually only the Hermit Thrush is present in eastern Pennsylvania during the winter. In summer the Hermit Thrush is rare near Philadelphia, but the Wood Thrush is common. Swainson's Thrush and the Gray-cheeked Thrush are seen during migration in spring and fall. Again, the maps in most field guides reflect this sort of information, and a detailed account of seasonal occurrence is contained in *A Field List of the Delaware Valley Region*, available from the Delaware Valley Ornithological Club, Academy of Natural Sciences, Philadelphia, Pennsylvania. A similar annotated list of birds seen at Peace Valley Park is available at the Nature Center.

Habitat, too, is important in identifying birds; even before you spot a bird you can know from the surroundings what species you are likely to see. Within its range a species usually is found only in certain habitats for which it has a preference and in many cases a degree of physical adaptation, although during migration some species stop over in different environments. As its name implies, the Marsh Wren is seldom found far from cattails, rushes, sedges, or tall marsh grasses, and if a wren-like bird is spotted in such a setting, it is unlikely to be a House Wren or Carolina Wren or one of the other species commonly found in thick underbrush or shrubbery. Similarly, ducks can be difficult to identify unless you tote a telescope; but even if all you can see is a silhouette, you can start with the knowledge that shallow marshes and creeks normally attract few diving ducks (such as Oldsquaw, Canvasbacks, Redheads, Ring-necked Ducks, Greater and Lesser Scaup, Common Goldeneye, and Buffleheads) and that large, deep bodies of water are not the usual setting for

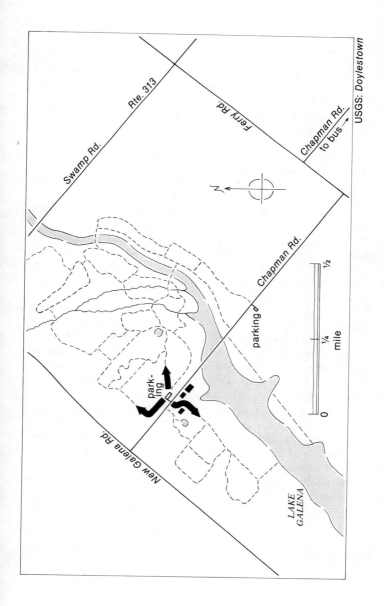

USGS: Doylestown

Rte. 313

Swamp Rd.

Ferry Rd.

Chapman Rd.
to bus

N

Chapman Rd.

parking

½   ¼
mile
0

park-
ing

New Galena Rd.

LAKE
GALENA

139

surface-feeding puddle ducks (American Black Duck, Gad-walls, Mallards, Common Pintails, American Widgeons, Wood Ducks, Northern Shovelers, and Blue-winged and Green-winged Teals).

Some of the distinctive habitats that provide a home to different bird species are: open ocean; beaches; sand dunes; salt marsh; mud flats; plowed fields; abandoned fields; meadows; thickets; moist, coniferous forests; dry, piney woods; bottom-land and upland deciduous forests; wooded swamps; ponds and creeks; clay banks; freshwater marshes; and open lakes, reservoirs, and estuaries. The area where two habitats join, called an ecotone, is a particularly good place to look for birds because of the likelihood that species peculiar to either environment will be present. For example, both meadowlarks and wood warblers might be found where a hay field abuts a forest. All good field guides provide information on habitat preference that may be used in locating specific species or in assessing the likelihood of a tentative identification.

Song also announces the identity (or at least the location) of birds even before they are seen. Some species, such as the Red-winged Blackbird, have only a few songs, while others, such as the Northern Mockingbird, have an infinite variety. Some birds — most notably thrushes — sing different songs in morning and evening. In many species the basic songs vary among individuals and also from one area to another, giving rise to regional "dialects." Nonetheless, the vocal repertory of most songbirds is sufficiently constant with respect to timbre and pattern that each species may be recognized simply by its songs.

Bird songs (as distinguished from calls) can be very complex and in most species are sung only by the male, usually in spring and summer. The male is the first to arrive at the breeding and nesting area after migration. He in effect stakes out a territory for courting, mating, and nesting by singing at prominent points around the area's perimeter, thus warding off intrusion by other males of his species and at the same time attracting females. On the basis of the male's display or the desirability of the territory he claims, the female selects her mate. In a few species, including Eastern Bluebirds, "Baltimore" Orioles, Northern Cardinals, and White-throated Sparrows, both sexes sing, although the males are more active in defending territory. Among mockingbirds, both sexes sing in fall and winter, but only the male sings in spring and summer.

Birds tend to heed the songs of their own kind and to ignore the songs of other species, which do not compete for females nor, in many cases, for the same type of nesting materials or food. In consequence, a single area might include the overlapping breeding territories of several species. From year to year such territories are bigger or smaller depending on the abundance or scarcity of food. Typically, most small songbirds require about ½ acre from which others of their species are excluded.

As for bird calls, they are short, sometimes harsh, and used by both males and females at all times of year to communicate alarm, aggression, location, and existence of food. Frequently, calls are heeded by many species, as in the case of warning calls, some of which are thin, high-pitched whistles that are difficult to locate and do not disclose the bird's position to predators. Birds also employ mobbing calls, used to summon other birds, as chickadees and crows do when scolding and harassing owls and other unwanted visitors. Birds flying in flocks, like Cedar Waxwings, often call continuously. Such calls help birds that migrate by night to stay together.

Finally, it should be noted that the phenomenon of bird dialects, and experiments with birds that have been deafened or raised in isolation, indicate that songs are genetically inherited only to a very crude extent. Young songbirds learn their songs by listening to adult birds and by engaging in practice, called *subsong*.

Probably the easiest way to learn bird songs is to listen repeatedly to recordings and simultaneously refer to a standard field guide. Most guides describe bird vocalizations with such terms as *harsh, nasal, flute-like, piercing, plaintive, wavering, twittering, buzzing, sneezy,* and *sputtering*. When played slowly, bird recordings demonstrate that the songs contain

141

many more notes than the human ear ordinarily hears.

Shape is one of the first and most important aspects to notice once you actually see a bird. Most birds can at least be placed in the proper family, and many species can be identified by shape or silhouette without reference to other field marks. Some birds, such as American Kestrels, are distinctly stocky, big-headed, and powerful looking, while others, such as Gray Catbirds and cuckoos, are more elegantly long and slender. Belted Kingfishers, Blue Jays, Tufted Titmice, Bohemian and Cedar Waxwings, and Northern Cardinals are among the small minority of birds with crests.

Bird bills frequently have distinctive shapes and show more adaptation to food supply than any other body part. The beak can be chunky like that of a grosbeak (which cracks seeds), thin and curved like that of a creeper (which probes bark for insects), hooked like that of a shrike (which tears at flesh), long and slender like that of a hummingbird (which sips nectar from tubular flowers), or some other characteristic shape depending on the bird's food. Goatsuckers, swifts, flycatchers, and swallows, all of which catch flying insects, have widely hinged bills and gaping mouths. The long, thin bills of starlings and meadowlarks are suited to probing the ground. In the Galapagos Islands west of Ecuador, Charles Darwin noted 14 species of finches, each of which had evolved a different type of beak or style of feeding that gave it a competitive advantage regarding a particular type of food.

In addition to beaks, nearly every other feature of a bird's body also shows adaptations that help it to exploit its environment successfully. Feet are significant: those of passerine species, or songbirds, are adapted to perching, with three toes in front and one long toe behind; waterfowl have webbed or lobed feet for swimming; and raptors have talons suited to grasping prey.

Other key elements of body shape are the length and form of wings, tails, and legs. Are the wings long, pointed, and developed for swift, sustained flight, like those of falcons? Or are the wings short and rounded for abrupt bursts of speed, like those of accipiters? Is the tail deeply forked like that of a Barn Swallow, shallowly notched like that of a Tree Swallow, square-tipped like that of a Cliff Swallow, round-tipped like that of a Blue Jay, pointed like that of a Mourning Dove, stubby like that of a European Starling, or long like that of a Brown Thrasher?

Size is of limited usefulness in identifying birds. Although size variation among birds of the same species is not great, size is difficult to estimate. The best approach for the bird watcher is to bear in mind the relative sizes of different species and to use certain well-known birds — chickadee, sparrow, robin, king-fisher, crow, and so forth — as standards for mental compari-son. For example, if a bird resembles a Song Sparrow but looks unusually large, it might be a Fox Sparrow.

Plumage, whether plain or princely, muted or magnificent, is one of the most obvious keys to identification. Color can occur in remarkable combinations of spots, stripes, streaks, patches, and other patterns that make even supposedly drab birds a pleasure to see. In some instances, like the brown streaks of American Bitterns and many other species, the plumage pro-vides camouflage. Most vireos and warblers are various shades and combinations of yellow, green, brown, gray, and black, as one would expect from their forest environment. The black and white backs of woodpeckers help them to blend in with bark dappled with sunlight. The bold patterns of Killdeers and some other plovers break up their outlines in much the same manner that warships used to be camouflaged. Many shore birds display countershading: they are dark above and light below, a pattern that reduces the effect of shadows and makes them appear an inconspicuous monotone. Even some brightly colored birds have camouflaging plumages when they are young and least able to avoid predators.

For some species, it is important *not* to be camouflaged. Many sea birds are mostly white, which in all light conditions enables them to be seen at great distances against the water. Because flocks of such birds spread out from their colonies to search for food, it is vital that a bird that has located food be visible to others after it has landed on the water to feed.

To organize the immense variation of plumages, focus on different basic elements. Starting with the head, is it uniformly colored as with the Red-headed Woodpecker? Is there a small patch on the crown, as with Wilson's Warbler or the Ruby-crowned Kinglet, or a larger cap on the front and top of the head, as with the Common Redpoll and American Goldfinch? Is the crown striped like that of an Ovenbird? Does a ring surround the eye, as with a Connecticut Warbler, or are the eye rings perhaps even joined across the top of the bill to form spectacles, as with a Yellow-breasted Chat? Is there a stripe over or through the eyes, as with the Red-breasted Nuthatch, or a conspicuous black mask across the eyes, like that of a Common Yellowthroat or Logger-head Shrike? From the head go on to the rest of the body, where distinctive colors and patterns can also mark a bird's bill, throat, breast, belly, back, sides, wings, rump, tail, and legs.

Finally, what a bird *does* is an important clue to its identity. Certain habits, postures, ways of searching for food, and other behavior are characteristic of different species. Some passerines, such as larks, juncos, and towhees, are strictly ground feeders; other birds, including flycatchers and swallows, nab insects on the wing; and still others, such as nuthatches and creepers, glean insects from the crevices in bark. Woodpeckers bore into the bark. Vireos and most warblers pick insects from the foliage of trees and brush. All these birds may be further distinguished by other habits of eating. For example, towhees scratch for insects and seeds by kicking backward with both feet together, whereas juncos rarely do, although both groups move on the ground by hopping. Still other ground feeders, such as meadowlarks, walk rather than hop. Swallows catch insects while swooping and skimming in continuous flight, whereas flycatchers dart out from a limb, grab an insect (sometimes with an audible smack), and then return to their perch. Brown Creepers have the curious habit of systematically searching for food by climbing trees in spirals, then flying back to the ground to climb again. Wood-peckers tend to hop upward, bracing themselves against the tree with their stiff tails. Nuthatches walk up and down trees and branches head first, seemingly without regard for gravity or blood pressure. Vireos are sluggish compared to the hyperactive, flitting warblers.

Many birds divide a food source into zones, apparently in an arrangement arrived at through evolution to ensure each species its own food supply. The short-legged Green Heron sits at the edge of water or on a low overhanging branch, waiting for its prey to come close to shore. The medium-sized Black-crowned Night Heron hunts in shallow water. The long-legged Great Blue Heron stalks fish in water up to 2 feet deep. Swans, geese, and many ducks graze underwater on the stems and tubers of grassy plants, but the longer necks of swans and geese enable them to reach deeper plants. Similarly, different species of shore birds take food from the same mud flat by probing with their varied bills to different depths. Various species of warblers that feed in the same tree are reported to concentrate in separate areas among the trunk, twig tips, tree top, and ground. Starlings and cowbirds feeding in flocks show another arrangement that provides an even distribution of food: those in the rear fly ahead to the front of the rank, so that the entire flock slowly rolls across the field.

Different species have not only different characteristic habits of feeding but also different styles of flight. Soaring is typical of some big birds. Gulls float nearly motionless in the wind. Buteos and Turkey Vultures glide on updrafts in wide circles, although Turkey Vultures may be further distinguished by the shallow V in which they hold their wings. Some other large birds, such as accipiters, rarely soar but instead interrupt their wing beats with glides. Kestrels, terns, and kingfishers can hover in one spot. Hummingbirds, like oversized dragonflies, also can hover and even fly backward. Slightly more erratic than the swooping, effortless flight of swallows is that of swifts, flitting with wing beats that appear to alternate (but do not). Still other birds, such as the American Goldfinch and flickers, dip up and down in wavelike flight. Some species, including jays and grackles, have no more imagination than to fly dead straight. Among ducks, the surface-feeding species launch themselves directly upward into flight, seeming to jump from the water, whereas the heavy diving ducks typically patter along the surface before becoming airborne.

Various idiosyncracies distinguish yet other species. The Spotted Sandpiper and Northern Waterthrush walk with a teetering, bobbing motion. Coots pump their heads back and forth as they swim. The Eastern Phoebe regularly jerks its tail downward while perching, whereas wrens often cock their tails vertically. Herons and egrets fly with their necks folded back; storks, ibises, and cranes fly with their necks outstretched. Still other birds have characteristic postures while sitting or flying or other unique habits that provide a reliable basis for identification.

*PUBLIC TRANSIT: From Olney station near the northern end of the Broad Street subway line, take SEPTA bus 55 to Doylestown. Get off at the Doylestown Shopping Center at the intersection of Main Street and Dublin Pike (also called East Street). You will know that your stop is coming after the bus passes through the center of Doylestown.*

*Doylestown is also served by train from Reading Terminal, but the Doylestown station is located 1 mile south of the Doylestown Shopping Center.*

*From the Doylestown Shopping Center, walk northwest on Dublin Pike past several roads. Cross over the Doylestown Bypass and continue to Pine Run Road. Turn left onto Pine Run Road, then right onto Chapman Road. Turn left onto Ferry Road, then right again onto Chapman Road. Continue to Lake Galena and the Peace Valley Nature Center. The walk from the shopping center is 2.4 miles.*

*AUTOMOBILE: From Philadelphia follow Route 611 (the northward extension of Broad Street) to Doylestown. Route 611 and Doylestown can also be reached from Exit 27 off the Pennsylvania Turnpike. As you approach Doylestown, circle west on the Doylestown Bypass (Route 611 Bypass). From the exit for Swamp Road (Route 313) north of Doylestown, turn northwest (left) onto Swamp Road and go 1 mile to Ferry Road. Turn left onto Ferry Road and follow it for 0.7 mile.*

*Turn right onto Chapman Road and go another 0.7 mile to the bridge at the eastern end of Lake Galena. The central parking lot for Peace Valley Nature Center is located a few hundred yards farther north opposite a barn and office.*

*THE WALK: Pick up a trail map from the box outside the Nature Center office. Referring to the map, any number of routes can be devised to suit your energy and curiosity. Although most of the trails are east of Chapman Road, do not miss the western section of the Nature Center where the trails overlook Lake Galena.*

Although Peace Valley Nature Center is part of the public park system of Bucks County, its programs are assisted by the Friends of Peace Valley Nature Center, Inc. For information about the center's activities write to Friends of PVNC, Inc., 170 Chapman Road, R.D. 1, Doylestown, Pennsylvania 18901.

## 15

# MILL GROVE

*Walking — 1 or more miles (1.6 or more kilometers). John James Audubon's first home in America. Overlooking Perkiomen Creek, an eighteenth-century stone house adjoins 130 acres of woods and meadow. Various paintings, drawings, and an original edition of* The Birds of America *— the four huge volumes of engraved, hand-colored prints that are the basis of Audubon's reputation — are on display in the house. Two of the rooms on the second floor are furnished in the style of the early 1800s. Stuffed birds and animals are also displayed. Open daily except Monday from 10:00 A.M. to 5:00 P.M. Closed New Year's Day, Thanksgiving, and Christmas. Dogs and picknicking are prohibited. Managed by the Montgomery County Park Board (666-5593).*

---

"**M**ILL GROVE was ever to me a blessed spot . . .," wrote John James Audubon, describing in later years his life there in 1804 – 1805. "For one year I was as happy as the young bird that, having left its parents' sight, carols merrily while hawks watch it for easy prey."

At the age of eighteen, Audubon had been sent from France to America, probably to escape conscription into Napoleon's army. Although born in San Domingo (now Haiti), the illegitimate son of a French sea captain and his French-Creole mistress, Audubon had been raised in his father's household in France by the captain's indulgent wife.

My stepmother who was devotedly attached to me completely spoiled me, hid my faults, boasted to everyone of my youthful

*Mill Grove house*

merits, and — worst of all — said frequently in my presence that I was the handsomest boy in France. All my wishes and idle notions were at once gratified. She went so far as actually to grant me *carte blanche* at all the confectionery spots in the town, and also in the village of Couëron, near Nantes, where we spent summers and eventually moved from the center of the city.

My father was of quite another, much more valuable turn of mind as to my welfare. He believed that the stores of the mind and not the power of gold coins render a man happy . . . . My father, long a seaman, and then in the French Republican Navy, wished me either to follow in his footsteps or to become an engineer. I studied drawing, geography, mathematics, fencing and the like, and also music for which I had considerable talent. Mathematics was hard dull work, I thought. Geography pleased me more. I was quite enthusiastic for dancing, and also for becoming commander of a corps of dragoons some day.

My father was mostly absent on duty, so that my mother let me do much as I pleased. Instead of applying closely to my studies I preferred to go with my friends in search of birds' nests, or to fish and shoot. I usually made for the field, my little basket filled with good eatables for lunch at school, but to burst with nests, eggs, lichens, flowers, and even pebbles from the shore of some rivulet by the time I came home at evening.

Audubon grew up undisciplined, spoiled, charming when he wanted to be, and at times given to neurotic fantasies and angry, irrational outbursts. He failed his examinations for officer's training. In later years he told his wife that he was the lost dauphin, Louis XVII, son of Louis XVI and Marie Antoinette.

When Audubon was sent to America, he stayed briefly with Miers Fisher, a wealthy Quaker. Fisher was business agent for Audubon's father for Mill Grove, a farm that the sea captain had bought years before as an investment. Audubon's father had asked Fisher to place his son (who at that time was named Jean Jacques, not John James) in a suitable household where he could learn English. Fisher responded by offering to have the boy stay with him at Urie, Fisher's handsome estate near Pennypack

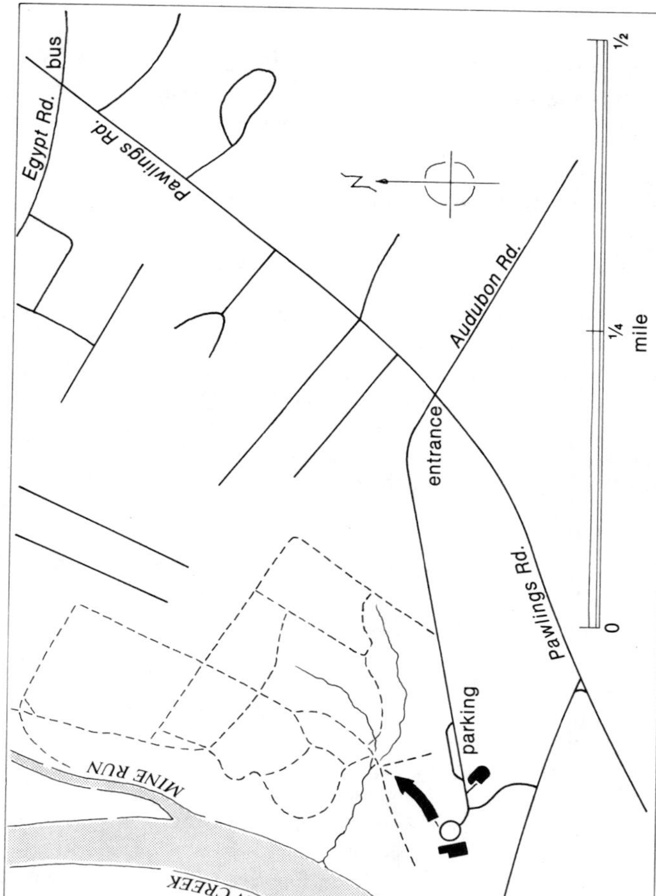

USGS: *Collegeville, Valley Forge*

Egypt Rd. bus

Pawlings Rd.

Audubon Rd.

entrance

Pawlings Rd.

parking

PERKIOMEN CREEK

MINE RUN

N

0    ¼    ½
        mile

151

Creek. Although Audubon later described Fisher as "kindly" and "good and learned," the sedate Quaker and young Frenchman did not get along. According to Audubon:

> [Fisher] was opposed to music of all descriptions, and dancing, and indeed to most of my amusements. He could not bear me to carry a gun or fishing-rod. At last I reminded him that it was a duty to install me on the estate to which my father had sent me.

Mill Grove was not at that time an "estate" but a working farm and gristmill, nor had Audubon's father sent him there. But Fisher complied with the young man's wishes, apparently glad to get rid of him. Audubon lived briefly with a family near Mill Grove, then later moved to Mill Grove itself as a boarder in the household of the farm's caretaker. Yet Audubon conducted himself as though he were the farm's owner: a young gentleman residing at his country seat.

> At Mill Grove I was presented to the caretaker and tenant farmer, William Thomas, also a Quaker. He was to dole out what was considered sufficient to a young gentleman's quarterly allowance . . .
>
> I pursued my simple and agreeable studies in Pennsylvania with as little concern about the future as if the world had been made for me. My rambles invariably commenced at break of day. To return, wet with dew, bearing a feathered prize, was and ever will be the highest enjoyment. Hunting, fishing, drawing and music occupied my every moment. Cares I knew not, and I cared naught about them. My neighbor and future father-in-law, William Bakewell of Fatland Ford plantation, a recent arrival from England, an excellent man and a great shot, often hunted with me. I was pleased to believe that his daughter Lucy looked upon me with some favor. His son Thomas was skating with me one morning on the Perkiomen, that first winter. He challenged me to shoot at his hat as he tossed it in the air while I passed at full speed. Accepting with great pleasure I went off like lightning — up and down — until the trigger was pulled. Down on the ice came the hat, as completely perforated as a sieve. He

repented (alas! too late) and was afterward severely reprimanded by Mr. Bakewell.

Fatland Ford is located on the east side of Pawlings Road ¼ mile south of the entrance to Mill Grove. The Bakewells moved there after Audubon's arrival at Mill Grove, but the young Frenchman refused to call on them, telling Mrs. Thomas that he did not wish to know anyone of the English race. But when he later met Bakewell while hunting, Audubon found the Englishman to be pleasant company and later, visiting at Fatland Ford, took an instant liking to his daughter. By the time Audubon left Mill Grove the following year, he and Lucy were engaged without their parents' approval. Audubon's father asked his business agent for information on the Bakewells, "their manners, conduct, means, and reason for being in that country . . . . Tell these good people that my son is not at all rich and that I can give him nothing if he marries in his present condition." The Bakewells, well-to-do gentry, were equally skeptical. Later, however, the parents agreed that their children could marry when they were older and John James was capable of supporting himself.

During his stay at Mill Grove, Audubon joined in a venture he thought would make him rich. With the aid of Francis Dacosta, who had replaced Miers Fisher as business agent, John James and William Thomas reopened an abandoned lead mine on the property. The mine, however, produced only violent disagreements between Audubon and Dacosta, who had acquired a half-interest in Mill Grove.

To the extent that Audubon did any other serious work at Mill Grove, it was his drawing:

When, as a little lad, I first represented birds on paper, I was under the impression that each sketch was a finished picture, because it possessed some sort of a head and tail and two sticks of legs. Oh! what bills and claws I did draw, to say nothing of a perfectly straight line for a back, and a tail stuck in, any way — like an unshipped rudder, and with never a thought of abutments to keep it from falling backward or forward. Many persons praised them to the skies. But my father constantly impressed upon me that nothing in the world possessing life and animation was easy to imitate, as I would gradually learn. I listened less to the others, and more to him; and his kind words and deep interest in my improvement became my law. My first collection of drawings — all stiff, unmeaning profiles — are such as one found in most such works. My next, begun in America, were from birds hung by a string tied to one foot, that I might show every portion as the wings lay loosely spread. In this manner I made some pretty fair signs for poulterers.

While watching the Pewees [Phoebes] and their graceful attitudes a thought struck my mind like a flash of light. Nothing, after all, could ever answer my enthusiastic desire to represent Nature, alive and moving, except to copy her in her own way. I began again. On I went, forming, literally, hundreds of outlines of my favorites, the Pewees. How good or bad I cannot tell, but I fancied I had mounted a step on the high pinnacle before me. I continued for months, simply outlining birds as I observed them, either alighted or on the wing. But I could finish none of my sketches. I lay many different species on the table or on the ground in attitudes for sketching. Alas! They were *dead,* to all intents and purposes, and neither wing, nor leg, nor tail could I place according to my wishes. Next I tried fastening threads to raise or lower a head, wing or tail, until I had something like life before me. Yet much was still wanting. When I saw the living birds I felt the blood rush to my temples. Almost in despair I spent about a month without drawing — deep in thought and daily in the company of the feathered inhabitants of Mill Grove.

I cogitated as to how far a manikin of a bird would answer. I labored with wood, cork and wires to form a figure, one so grotesque that when set up it was like a tolerable-looking Dodo. A friend roused my ire by laughing at it immoderately, assuring me that if I wished to represent a tame gander it might do. I gave it a kick, broke it to atoms, walked off, and thought again.

Young as I was, and impatient, I let my desire fill my brains with many plans. Not infrequently I dreamed I had made a new discovery. One morning long before day I leaped out of bed, ordered a horse to be saddled, mounted it, and went off at a gallop towards

Norristown, about five miles away. Not a door was yet open. I went to the river, took a bath, returned to the town, entered the first open shop, bought wire of different sizes, leaped on my steed and was soon again at Mill Grove. I really believe my tenant's wife thought I was mad. On being offered my breakfast, I told her I only wanted my gun. I was off to the creek, shot the first Kingfisher I met, carried it home by the bill, sent for the miller, and had him bring me a piece of soft board. When he returned with it he found me filing sharp points on wire, ready to show him what I meant to do.

I pierced the body to fix it on the board, passed a second wire above the upper mandible to hold the head in a pretty fair attitude, and with finer wires arranged the feet according to my notions. Even common pins came to my assistance. The last wire delightfully elevated the tail, and at last — there stood before me the *real* Kingfisher. The lack of breakfast was not at all in my way. No, indeed! I outlined the bird with the aid of compasses, then colored and finished it without a thought of hunger. My honest miller stood by, delighted to see me so pleased. This was what I shall call my first drawing actually from Nature, for even the model's eye was still as if full of life when I pressed the lids aside with my finger.

For the rest of his life Audubon used this method to pose birds for drawing.

Audubon returned to France in the middle of 1805. A year later he was back at Mill Grove in company with Ferdinand Rosier. The fathers of Audubon and Rosier had established their sons in business as informal partners. They were empowered to settle business differences with Dacosta and to sell Mill Grove, which they did. Audubon then spent half a year playing at business in New York before moving to Kentucky with Rosier to start a general store in Louisville. In 1808 Audubon traveled to Fatland Ford, married Lucy Bakewell, and returned with her to Louisville.

Two years later, while Audubon and Rosier were in their store, a stranger walked in carrying two large volumes. It was Alexander Wilson (discussed in Chapter 9), who was in Louisville collecting bird specimens and selling orders for his *Ameri-*

*can Ornithology,* of which the first two volumes had been completed. Each bird was portrayed in a color plate and described in the accompanying text. Audubon was about to purchase a set when Rosier told him that he was foolish to buy someone else's pictures when his own were so much better.

Some biographers date the inception of Audubon's own monumental project, *The Birds of America,* from this encounter with Wilson. In any event, after successive business reverses, Audubon spent the period between 1820 and 1826 traveling and drawing birds. Lucy taught school while her husband earned money as an itinerant portrait painter and instructor of dancing and fencing. In 1826, after he had failed to find a publisher or patron in America, Audubon took his bird paintings to England, where he was acclaimed immediately. Having secured a publisher, he worked continuously and brilliantly for twelve years, monitoring the engravers and colorists, writing text, promoting his project, and traveling to find and paint additional birds. Printed in double elephant-size folios (an open volume measures 40 by 52 inches) and containing 435 life-sized color plates, the four volumes of *The Birds of America* appeared between 1827 and 1838. This work was followed by a popular edition of smaller prints and then by *The Viviparous Quadrupeds of North America,* written in collaboration with John Bachman and completed by Audubon's sons after their father's death in 1851.

As for Mill Grove, it was acquired by Samuel Wetherill of Philadelphia in 1813 and remained in the Wetherill family until its sale to Montgomery County in 1951.

*PUBLIC TRANSIT: From Reading Terminal take the train to DeKalb Street in Norristown. Alternatively, from 69th Street Terminal or from the western suburbs, take the Norristown High-Speed Line (SEPTA 100) to Norristown.*

*From Norristown take SEPTA bus 98 via Main Street, Marshall Street, and Egypt Road to the intersection of Egypt Road and Park Avenue in the center of the village of Audubon. (South of this intersection, Park Avenue changes name to Pawlings Road.) You will know that your stop is coming* when the bus passes Crawford Road and then Orchard Lane on the right.

From the bus stop in the center of Audubon, walk ½ mile south on Pawlings Road to the entrance to Mill Grove on the right.

AUTOMOBILE: Mill Grove is located just south of the village of Audubon and north of Valley Forge National Historic Park. From Philadelphia take the Schuylkill Expressway (I-76) to Exit 26 for Route 202 west to Paoli. After about ½ mile leave Route 202 at the exit for Betzwood Bridge. Follow the highway north past Valley Forge and across the Schuylkill River, then exit immediately for Trooper Road (Route 363). Turn left onto Audubon Road at the first traffic light. Follow Audubon Road 1.1 miles to an intersection with Pawlings Road. The entrance to Mill Grove is straight ahead on the far side of the intersection.

Alternatively, from the center of Audubon, Mill Grove is south 0.5 mile on Pawlings Road. The entrance is on the right and is marked by stone posts.

THE WALK: First visit Audubon's house and the meadow sloping down to the river. Then, with your back toward the front door, bear half-left across the driveway and onto a footpath leading across the lawn and into the woods. At a trail junction cross a small footbridge, then turn left. Continue through the woods and along the edge of the steep valley bordering Perkiomen Creek and Mine Run. Turn right at a grassy path bordering dense, scrubby woods, or (for a longer walk) continue several hundred yards to the next right-hand intersection. Return through woods and meadow.

# 16

# VALLEY FORGE NATIONAL HISTORIC PARK

*Walking and ski touring — 6.5 miles (10.5 kilometers). An expanse of rolling meadows and wooded hills where the Continental Army camped during the winter of 1777-1778. From the visitor center the route follows the outer line of defense, where reconstructed earthworks and log huts occupy the crest of a low ridge. Continue along Valley Creek to Washington's headquarters at the Isaac Potts house. Return through the fields of the Grand Parade. The visitor center and Washington's headquarters are open daily except Christmas from 8:30 A.M. to 5:00 P.M. Dogs must be leashed. Telephone for information about bicycle rental. Managed by the National Park Service (783-7700).*

---

THE ARMY WAS NOW not only starved but naked. The greatest part were not only shirtless and barefoot, but destitute of all other clothing, expecially blankets. I procured a small piece of raw cowhide and made myself a pair of moccasins, which kept my feet (while they lasted) from the frozen ground, although, as I well remember, the hard edges so galled my ankles while on a march, that it was with much difficulty and pain that I could wear them afterwards; but the only alternative I had was to endure this inconvenience or to go barefoot, as hundreds of my companions had to, till they might be tracked by their blood upon the rough frozen ground. But hunger, nakedness and sore shins were not the only difficulties we had at this time to encounter; we had hard duty to perform and little or no strength to perform it with.

*Inner line of defense*

So wrote Private Joseph Plumb Martin, describing the condition of the Continental Army during December 1777, immediately before the Americans' withdrawal to Valley Forge. Early in September the British forces under General Sir William Howe had landed at the northern end of Chesapeake Bay. In a series of battles, marches, and counter-marches during the following weeks, the Continental Army under George Washington had been defeated and outmaneuvered. On September 11 the Americans at Chadds Ford on Brandywine Creek had failed to stop the northward advance of the British. Feinting first toward Washington's supply depot at Reading, Howe's forces then crossed the Schuylkill River and occupied Germantown and Philadelphia, the seat of Congress, which had fled westward to Lancaster. At Germantown on October 4, the British repulsed an attack by the Americans. While the Continental Army took up positions near Whitemarsh (site of present-day Fort Washington Park), the British forced the Americans to abandon Forts Mifflin and Mercer on the Delaware River below Philadelphia, thus opening the city to their supply ships.

By mid-December the British were ensconced for the winter in Philadelphia, while the American army, after several days of ineffectual marching backward and forward, was starving at a temporary encampment at Gulph Mills. There the army observed a belated Continental Thanksgiving that had been ordered by Congress. In some regiments the supplies issued by the commissary were so meager as to seem a perverse joke. Wrote Private Martin:

> But we must now have what Congress said, a sumptuous Thanksgiving to close the year of high living we had now nearly seen brought to a close. Well, to add something extraordinary to our present stock of provisions, our country, ever mindful of its suffering army, opened her sympathizing heart so wide, upon this occasion, as to give us something to make the world stare. And what do you think it was, reader? Guess. You cannot guess, be you as much of a Yankee as you will. I will tell you; it gave each and every man *half* a gill [i.e., ¼ cup] of rice and a *tablespoonful* of vinegar!!

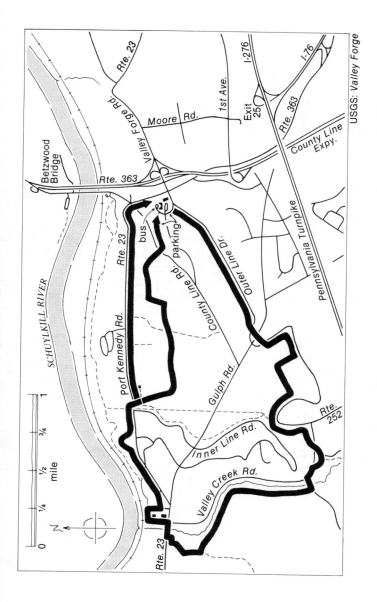

USGS: Valley Forge

161

On December 19 the American army at Gulph Mills marched west 6 miles to Valley Forge, which had been selected as the site for the winter encampment. About 18 miles from Philadelphia, Valley Forge was too remote for the British to reach with a swift surprise attack, yet close enough for the Americans to harass British units trying to obtain supplies from the farms and agricultural communities north and west of the city. It was thought that this same farmland would help to supply food for the American army. Also, the terrain surrounding Valley Forge was defensible. A long, low ridge faced the southeast; the Schuylkill River protected the north; and the west was dominated by the high hills of Mount Misery and Mount Joy.

Valley Forge itself was an iron-making community — or at least had been until a few months prior to the arrival of the Continental Army. Owned jointly by Isaac Potts and his brother-in-law William Dewees, Valley Forge had helped to supply munitions to the Americans. According to one account, a hundred men had been employed working fourteen hours a day. On September 18, however, the community was occupied by the British, who seized the supplies that were stored there and burned the forge and a sawmill before moving on to Philadelphia. A gristmill was left intact.

When the American forces reached Valley Forge, the army consisted of approximately 12,000 men — that is, about 17 percent of the crowd that nowadays regularly fills Philadelphia's Veterans Stadium to watch the Eagles play football. Of these, 2,898 men were found to be unfit for duty on December 23 because they lacked shoes or clothes. The army's supply of flour totaled twenty-five barrels. There were virtually no cattle suitable for eating. Describing his first full day at Valley Forge, Private Martin wrote:

> I lay here two nights and one day and had not a morsel of anything to eat all the time, save half of a small pumpkin, which I cooked by placing it upon a rock, the skin side uppermost, and making a fire upon it. By the time it was heat through I devoured it with as keen an appetite as I should a pie made of it at some other time.

On December 21 the chant, "No meat, no meat" spread through the camp, and Washington was convinced that a mutiny was imminent. Two days later he wrote that "unless some great and capital change suddenly takes place in the Commissary Department this Army must inevitably be reduced to one or the other of three things: starvation, dissolution or dispersal in order to obtain subsistence in the best manner it can."

By the end of December, 6 inches of snow covered the ground. Foraging parties were ordered into the countryside to collect food. Private Martin, who was among those sent out, described his duty as "plundering — sheer privateering," and as "nothing more nor less than to procure provisions from the inhabitants for the men in the army and forage for the poor perishing cattle belonging to it, at the point of the bayonet." In return for their goods, farmers were given certificates supposedly entitling them to reimbursement and to relief from further requisitions. Even payment in cash was dubious compensation since the army used the debased paper currency issued by the national government.

Starting February 9, daily markets to which farmers brought supplies were held at the edge of camp. Washington wrote, "Prices have been affixed by handbills and they are to be strictly observed. However, British currency may prove more attractive to the farmers than our Continental monies and it remains whether patriotism will conquer greed." To prevent commerce with the British, Congress granted the American army authority to try civilians who supplied goods to the enemy, and twenty-one farmers and merchants were in fact convicted at Valley Forge.

Food, clothes, blankets, medicines, and virtually all other materials necessary for the maintenance and refurbishment of the army continued in short supply throughout the winter. By February 5 the number of men unable to report for duty because of the lack of shoes or clothes had swelled to 3,989. Sentries at times stood on their hats to protect their feet from the cold ground. The troops frequently went without meat, sometimes for as long as a week. Farmers in the vicinity of the camp hid their cattle. The only staple appears to have been "firecake," a mixture of flour and water baked on a griddle. The soldiers' pay was several months in arrears. Desertions occurred almost daily.

The shortages did not reflect a general scarcity of goods in Pennsylvania or in other states. Rather, poor transportation and inefficient procurement restricted the flow of supplies: roads were nearly impassable, and wagon contractors and teamsters were unwilling to work for the wages authorized by Congress. For example, on February 14, one general noted that "the Commissioners have found a quantity of pork in Jersey, of which by a failure of wagons, not one barrel has reached the camp." The Schuylkill River froze early in January and was not navigable by barges until late March. The states, responsible for recruiting troops, were also supposed to supply them with uniforms and equipment, but the state and local governments were slow to act. Also, popular support was never mobilized because of the desire to keep the weakness and impoverishment of the army a secret from the enemy.

For the mass of the army, the main task after arriving at Valley Forge was to build winter shelters. Before leaving Gulph Mills, Washington had ordered the formation of twelve-man squads. Each squad was to erect its own hut made of logs chinked with clay, and most were completed by the end of January. Although snug, the huts were poorly ventilated and frequently damp and smoky. General Lafayette termed them "little shanties that are scarcely gayer than dungeon cells." When spring arrived, orders were issued to the squads to make the huts as "airy as possible" by removing the chinking from between the logs, and each hut was "purified" daily by burning in it a musket cartridge or a bit of tar. Replicas of some of the huts stand throughout the park.

The huts were built adjacent to the defensive positions assigned to the troops. An inner line of defense ran along the eastern and southern slopes of Mount Joy. By the end of April the inner line consisted of a long dry-moat backed by an earthen mound and secured at each end by artillery emplacements.

Several hundred yards in front of the trench, a line of sharpened stakes (called abatis) slanted forward. An outer line of defense, which was never fully completed, stretched westward along the ridge from the present site of the visitor center. Crossing the midpoint of this line was Gulph Road, thought to be the most likely approach for the British. Earthworks were also built overlooking a bridge that eventually was constructed across the Schuylkill River.

Most of the army's cannons were massed in the Artillery Park at the center of the camp. From there the cannons could be sent to any point under attack — but attack never occurred. General Howe reported to London that the position of the Continental Army was too strong for him to take during winter weather, and by spring the American position was stronger still.

Throughout the winter, disease gripped much of the American army. An estimated two thousand to three thousand soldiers died of pneumonia, dysentery, typhoid, and typhus, the last two diseases then known as "putrid fever." Sickness was aggravated by lack of food, inadequate clothing, and crowded conditions in the huts. Sanitation was poor. On January 7 Washington ordered "all dead horses in and about the Camp, and all offal, to be burned." He noted the "filth and nastiness" near some of the huts. Five lashes were ordered for "any soldier who shall fail to ease himself anywhere but at a proper Necessary." On February 20 General Joseph Reed noted that "sickness and mortality have spread through the quarters of the Soldiers to an astonishing degree." Hospitals were established in the outlying communities, but the influx of enfeebled troops filled them to two or three times their intended capacity. Shortages and ignorance caused newly arrived patients to be issued blankets and bed straw previously used by men who had died of contagious diseases.

Even relatively healthy soldiers were plagued by scabies, lice, and other vermin. Private Martin described how he and his mates rubbed themselves with a mixture of tallow and sulphur: "We killed the itch and we were satisfied, for it had almost killed us. This was a decisive victory, the only one we had achieved lately." A mocking article in a Tory newspaper noted the large quantity of "meat" to be found crawling on the backs of the Continental soldiers and suggested that it might be a solution for the army's short rations.

Probably the principal accomplishment at Valley Forge was the development of a new program of military training. The army had been hampered on march and in battle by its inability to move quickly in compact formations. The troops knew how to march only in single file. Changing to combat formations or from one position in battle to another took an inordinate length of time, and the troops often became confused. Coordination was difficult even among those troops which had received training, since units from different states had been instructed in different systems and formations.

The person most responsible for supervising the training of the troops was Inspector General Thomas Conway, but Washington did not trust him or follow his suggestions because Conway and others had been trying to discredit Washington with Congress. Eventually Conway was replaced by Friedrich von Steuben, an unemployed Prussian officer who had been recommended to Congress by Benjamin Franklin, America's ambassador in Paris. Von Steuben arrived at Valley Forge on February 23, 1778, and was assigned by Washington to inspect several regiments and to recommend steps to correct whatever problems he found. Favorably impressed with von Steuben's plan of remedial training, Washington appointed him acting inspector general.

Von Steuben's first step was to write a simplified manual of drill procedures to be applied to the entire army. Because von Steuben spoke little English, this document had to be translated. Day by day, as each installment was completed, copies were made by newly appointed brigade inspectors.

Von Steuben selected a unit composed partly of Washington's Life Guards — a select body of soldiers, chosen from the ranks by the general himself to serve as his personal guard — as a model for the rest of the army. Von Steuben personally instructed these men, at times taking a musket in his own hands in the manner of a drill sergeant to demonstrate his simplified manual of arms and routinized procedure for reloading. After looking on, the brigade inspectors returned to their troops and taught the rest of the army. Separate squads of "awkward troops" were formed for recruits or other soldiers slow to learn the new maneuvers. On April 8 Washington noted, "Our Army, heretofore slovenly and ragged, now is becoming more military."

Von Steuben imposed a standard tempo of marching and a standard stride. He taught the troops to march in columns, to move from columns to combat lines facing the enemy, to wheel in line on the battlefield, and to regroup. He instructed them in the use of the bayonet, for which the British had been feared. (Von Steuben had noticed those Americans who had bayonets using them chiefly as skewers to broil meat.) He reorganized the forces into units of standard size and reallocated weapons to provide a greater degree of uniformity within each company. In short, von Steuben taught the troops to march, shoot, and charge as units, as was required for effective use of the inaccurate muskets and the bayonet. Private Martin commented, "After I had joined my regiment I was kept constantly, when off other duty, engaged in learning the Baron de Steuben's new Prussian exercises. It was a continual drill."

Many officers at first were dismayed by von Steuben's attention to detail and his (as they thought) demeaning habit of working directly with the troops. According to military custom of the day, an officer's only duty toward his men was to lead them in combat or patrol. During the inactivity of winter, many officers had applied to go home on furlough, but von Steuben's example prompted them to undertake a wider range of responsibility toward the troops. Also, hundreds of officers who had resigned or been dismissed during the winter were replaced with more dedicated men.

With the coming of spring, the army's physical condition, morale, training, and equipment steadily improved. Supplies of food reached the camp more regularly, and by March cattle were being butchered daily. In April the troops caught and salted an immense haul of shad during the annual run on the Schuylkill

River. Fresh troops arrived. New muskets were obtained and old ones repaired. Bayonets — which had been issued to only half of the Americans — were manufactured. Teams of draft animals were again assembled. Clothing, shoes, and other supplies came from France and from the states. On May 1 Washington wrote, "Daily this Army looks more like a military force and less like an armed horde." On May 6, 1778, the new alliance with France was celebrated formally by the assembled army.

Soon word reached the camp that the British were preparing to abandon Philadelphia. After half a year they had accomplished virtually nothing, while allowing the Americans to regain and surpass their earlier strength and to forge an effective, well-organized army, which now prepared feverishly to take to the field. On June 18 news arrived that during the night the British had left Philadelphia headed toward New York. By the end of the afternoon, one American division was in pursuit. The rest of the army marched away from Valley Forge the following day, six months exactly after they had limped into their winter encampment.

*PUBLIC TRANSIT:    From Kennedy Boulevard between 16th and 17th streets (just north of Penn Center), take SEPTA bus 45 to King of Prussia Plaza and Valley Forge via Market Street, the Schuylkill Expressway, and South Gulph Road. Get off at the end of the line at the visitor center for Valley Forge National Historic Park.*

*AUTOMOBILE:    From Philadelphia take the Schuylkill Expressway (I-76) to Exit 25 for Route 363 and Valley Forge. Circle right, then follow Route 363 north for 1.8 miles to an intersection with Route 23. Turn left into the park.*

*From east or west on the Pennsylvania Turnpike, take Exit 24 for Valley Forge. Stay in the right-hand lane for the toll booth, then immediately turn right at Exit 25 for Route 363 and Valley Forge. Follow Route 363 north for 1.5 miles to an intersection with Route 23. Turn left into the park.*

*From east or west on Route 202, take the Valley Forge —*

Betzwood Bridge exit. Proceed 1.5 miles to the exit for Route 23 west and Valley Forge. Follow Route 23 west 0.1 mile to the park entrance.

From the north follow Trooper Road (Route 363) across the Schuylkill River, then exit immediately for Route 23 and Valley Forge.

THE WALK:    From the Valley Forge visitor center follow the bicycle path that starts on the far side of the entrance road opposite the end of the stone administration building. Follow the path along the park's southern ridge past the recon-structed huts of the Muhlenberg Brigade and other units of the Continental Army. Eventually cross two roads in order to pass under the National Memorial Arch. Continue downhill on the far side of the arch, cross the road, and turn left onto the bicycle path. Continue to a parking lot and picnic area, then follow the paved path to the right away from the road and around the edge of the woods. (During fall and winter, when ticks are not a problem, you may prefer to proceed from Memorial Arch straight across the road and meadow to the path along the edge of the woods.)

Continue right where the bicycle path rejoins the park road. Pass through an intersection with a gravel road where the park road veers downhill to the left. Bear left as the path also turns downhill. Turn right near the bottom of the slope. Cross Valley Creek Road (Route 252) and follow the bicycle path to its end below a parking lot.

From the end of the bicycle path, continue on the gravel drive of Valley Forge Farm. Pass a driveway intersecting from the left, then bear right between farm buildings. Rejoin Valley Creek Road and follow it downhill 140 yards to an intersection with a road and covered bridge over Valley Creek. Cross the bridge, then immediately turn right onto the riverside footpath. With the creek on the right, follow the path downstream past a bridge and the site of William Dewees's Upper Forge (as opposed to Valley Forge farther downstream). Continue as the path slants uphill to the left *and then turns right. Where the path emerges at a grassy clearing, bear right downhill to a house, then follow the driveway downhill. At Valley Forge Road turn right across Valley Creek. At an intersection 60 yards beyond the bridge, turn left across the road. Follow a wide gravel drive past the William Dewees house to Washington's headquarters at the Isaac Potts house.*

At the outset of the Valley Forge encampment, Washington — who had promised his soldiers to "share in the Hardships and partake of every inconvenience" — lived in a tent. He soon found, however, that his responsibilities required use of a house. For a hundred pounds, he rented the Isaac Potts house from the widow of one of Isaac's brothers. Nearby he had a log shelter built where he, his aides, and officers dined. Other generals stayed in farmhouses near the camp.

Behind the Potts house were the huts of Washington's forty-six Life Guards. On March 11, 1776, Washington had ordered the commanding officer of each regiment to recommend four native-born soldiers, men of "sobriety, honesty and good behavior . . . handsomely and well made . . . neat and spruce." From the total, Washington picked a guard for himself and his baggage.

Across Valley Creek from Washington's headquarters were the camps and shops of the Artificers — men whose duty it was to repair muskets, make bayonets, and perform similar tasks. Nearby, the Dewees house was called the "Bakehouse" because ovens were installed in the basement.

*Continue around the Potts house past the former railroad station. Turn right past the reconstructed huts of Washington's Life Guards. At the parking area rejoin the bicycle path running uphill along Port Kennedy Road. Eventually cross the road where the statue of Major General Friedrich Wilhelm Baron von Steuben comes into view on the right. The statue overlooks the broad meadow of the Grand Parade, where von Steuben directed the army in basic field drills and battle maneuvers. From the parking area near the statue, follow a footpath 125 yards to the stone farmhouse that served as General James Varnum's quarters.*

*From the statue of von Steuben, the bicycle path follows Port Kennedy Road along the park's northern ridge back to the visitor center. A more agreeable route during fall and winter, when ticks are not a problem, is to descend into the Grand Parade, then gradually bear left through the middle of the meadow. Follow the bottom of the valley toward a row of distant evergreen trees. Pass far below the spire of Washington Memorial Chapel, located at the top of the left ridge. Eventually follow the edge of the evergreens uphill to the left. About 100 yards below the crest of the ridge, turn right onto a dirt road leading into the woods. Pass through a pine plantation. Continue downhill to join a gravel road. At an intersection with County Line Road, bear half-left across the road and enter the lower parking area for the visitor center. Continue left through the parking lot to reach the visitor center itself and the upper parking lot.*

# 17

# HOPEWELL VILLAGE

*Walking — 1 or more miles (1.6 or more kilometers). A small iron-making village, including a stone furnace, water wheel and bellows, casting house, office and store, blacksmith shop, sheds, barn, tenant houses and ironmaster's residence — all restored or reconstructed to their early nineteenth-century appearance. Paths lead a short distance to Hopewell Lake in adjoining French Creek State Park, where there are camping, picnicking, and swimming facilities and an extensive trail system. Hopewell Village National Historic Site is open daily from 9:00 A.M. to 5:00 P.M. Closed Christmas and New Year's Day. Dogs must be leashed. Picnicking is prohibited in Hopewell Village. Managed by the U.S. National Park Service (582-8773). French Creek State Park is managed by the Pennsylvania Bureau of State Parks (582-1514).*

---

NEW ORLEANS VICTORY STOVE, Perry Victory Stove, Don't Give Up the Ship Stove, Decatur Flat Front Stove, and Peace Stove: these were just a few of the iron products cast at Hopewell in the years of patriotic fervor following the War of 1812. As the war receded into the past, new stove motifs appeared: the Flower Pot, Hornet and Peacock, Foxchase, and Shepherd. By 1832 the village was producing ninety-eight different stove patterns in cylindrical, oval, square, and other shapes. Some were adapted for burning coal instead of wood. A few models were patented; some bore the name Hopewell, others the names of retailers who supplied their own patterns.

Annual production exceeded three thousand stoves. During the "long blast" of 1836–37, when the furnace was kept in

*Furnace complex*

continuous operation for 445 days, 720 tons of castings were made; all but a few tons were stove parts. During the same period 449 tons of pig iron were produced. At that time Hopewell was at the peak of its prosperity, employing more than 160 miners, woodcutters, colliers, teamsters, molders, and other hands. The village was an "iron plantation" — a single enterprise with its own farms, forests, open pit mines, water source, dwellings, store, and other structures, all supporting the operation of the small stone furnace.

The furnace at Hopewell was built about 1771 at a time when there were more than fifty iron furnaces and forges in Pennsylvania. The furnaces — fat masonry stacks, typically resembling steep little pyramids — were hollow and lined with firebrick. Water-powered bellows provided an intermittent blast of air that, with a heavy, pulsing roar, fanned the furnace fire. The rush of air was called a *cold-blast* because the air was not preheated, as it was in the *hot-blast* technology developed later. Other requisites were charcoal fuel made from cordwood (the only fuel suitable for cold-blast furnaces), limestone flux to coagulate impurities in the ore, and of course the ore itself. All of these ingredients could be obtained near Hopewell Village, which, like other iron-making communities of the day, was located in an extensive tract of forest far from any major city.

Usually the furnaces were built near the bottom of a steep slope with a bridge running from the crest of the bank to the top of the stack. Iron ore, charcoal, and limestone were carted across the bridge and dumped into the top of the stack, which also served as the chimney. The stack gases were nearly smokeless, but occasionally streams of sparks shot out, and at night flames lit the sky and surrounding buildings. The higher of two taps in the furnace was opened regularly to draw off the slag that floated on the molten iron, which slowly sank to the crucible at the bottom of the stack. Then two or three times a day the lower tap was opened and the liquid iron poured into molds.

The molds might consist of nothing more than short, parallel troughs branching from a central channel dug in the sandy floor of the casting house, which was a barnlike structure built around

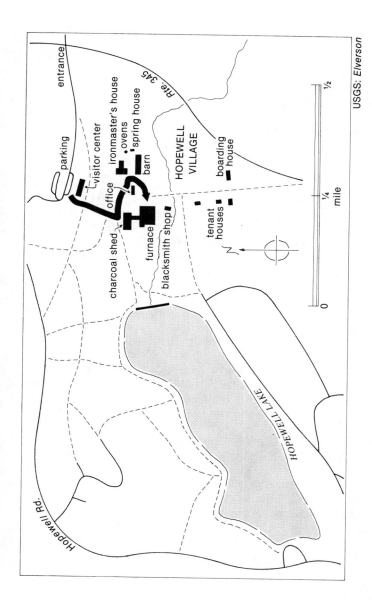

USGS: Elverson

entrance

Rte. 345

parking

visitor center

ironmaster's house

ovens

spring house

office

barn

HOPEWELL VILLAGE

boarding house

charcoal shed

furnace

blacksmith shop

tenant houses

N

Hopewell Rd.

HOPEWELL LAKE

0   ¼   ½
mile

175

the furnace. In the early days of iron manufacturing, the main pouring channel and the row of smaller molds were noted to resemble a sow with suckling pigs; hence the term *pig iron* for crude iron. The molds might also consist of patterns pressed into the sand in order to produce *open sand* casts, which were puddles of iron molded only on the lower surface. Early stove panels were made this way. Later, *flask* casting — which requires a two-sided hollow mold — was used to mold pieces more precisely on all surfaces.

The proprietors of Hopewell Village owned thousands of acres of surrounding forest from which wood for charcoal was cut. Lumbering was done during winter. Cut into 4-foot lengths, the logs were hauled on sleds to charcoal hearths — large circular clearings — scattered throughout the forest. There the wood was left to dry until late spring. The colliers then arranged the logs in a circular mass 30 or 40 feet in diameter, with all the pieces standing on end and leaning toward a wooden chimney at the center. Another smaller layer was stacked on top of the first, and a third layer over that, until a rounded heap of wood was built. Then the colliers covered the logs with a layer of leaves and dirt. The chimney was filled with kindling and a fire set at the top.

For as long as two weeks the colliers watched over the mound while the wood smouldered and turned to charcoal. Outbreaks of flame were quickly smothered with dirt. Blue smoke indicated that all was going well, but white smoke was a sign of too much combustion. The rate of charring was controlled by opening and filling air holes. The most dangerous part of the job was "jumping the pit," which entailed climbing on top of the smoking heap and stamping on it to settle the coals and fill in air spaces. Finally, when the charring appeared to be complete, the colliers uncovered the mound a little at a time. The hot charcoal was loaded into metal-lined wagons, which then were hauled to the village and parked in a shed to protect the coals from rain. After the charcoal had cooled, it was added to the supplies stored in the charcoal house.

Once adequate supplies of charcoal, ore, and limestone were

accumulated at the village, the furnace was *put in blast* — that is, ignited for the year. The furnace was kept in blast until the furnace lining deteriorated to the point where it needed replacement or until the supplies were exhausted. Usually the first item to run out was charcoal, because it could not be manufactured and replenished during winter.

While the furnace was in blast, workmen known as fillers dumped fresh charges of charcoal, ore, and limestone into the furnace every half hour around the clock. Each charge consisted of about 15 bushels of charcoal, 200 to 300 pounds of ore, and several shovelfuls of limestone. In general, production of a ton of iron consumed 1 or 2 tons of charcoal, 2 tons of ore, and a few hundred pounds of limestone. The daily output was between 3 and 4 tons of iron.

Working in the casting shed, the founder could monitor the quality of the iron, which to some extent could be controlled by adjusting the proportion of ingredients and the blast of air. When the time came to tap the furnace, the founder rang a bell to summon the molders, who then ladled the molten iron into molds they had prepared since the last casting. The founder was paid according to the quality and quantity of the iron he produced, and the molders according to the number, intricacy, and quality of their castings. Sometimes women earned money by cleaning the castings and filing off fins of extra metal produced by the seams in the molds. Most castings were sent unassembled to the retailers, although some stoves and other articles were bolted together at Hopewell and sold in the company store.

Aside from the furnace complex (consisting of the furnace itself, the water wheel, bellows, casting house, cleaning shed, bridge, and charcoal house), the other structures at Hopewell Village are the company store, the ironmaster's residence, the tenant houses, and the barn for the village draft animals. The store sold food staples and general merchandise to the workers. Some employees who lived in the village had their own garden plots, chickens, hogs, and cows. Workers could also buy produce grown in the village fields, which were leased to share-croppers. The store doubled as the company office, where records were kept detailing orders for iron products, output of the furnace, and each worker's earnings and debts.

The ironmaster's residence was called the Big House. A large dining room and kitchen in the basement provided meals (for a fee) to men who were unmarried or working away from home.

At the peak of Hopewell's prosperity, at least fourteen tenant houses existed in the village and were leased to workers. Rent was deducted from the tenants' earnings. Some of the houses were small, single-family structures; others were dormitories for single men. Several tenant houses were located near the company mines. Many workers lived in their own houses near the village and walked to the furnace each day or slept in various outbuildings between shifts.

Although Hopewell's best years were in the first half of the nineteenth century, the furnace had been a significant source of cannon, shot, and other iron munitions during the Revolutionary War. Mark Bird, who built the furnace and whose father (also an ironmaster) gave his name to nearby Birdsboro, was a leading patriot. In the autumn of 1777 Mark Bird fitted out three hundred soldiers with uniforms, tents, and provisions at his own expense, and in February 1778 he sent a thousand barrels of flour to Valley Forge. Bird owned several furnaces and foundries, and his workers were discharged from the militia during the war so that they could continue to produce munitions.

After the Revolution, however, Bird's fortunes crashed. Large debts owed him by the Continental Congress went unpaid or were discharged in depreciated currency. Hopewell's furnace was flooded and closed. Another of Bird's furnaces burned. Bird borrowed heavily but was unable to repay, so in 1788 his properties were auctioned at a sheriff's sale. "There is no doubt my principle ruin was by the Warr & Depretiation . . .," Bird wrote in later years.

After a succession of owners during the 1790s, Hopewell was acquired in 1800 by the partnership of Matthew Brooke, his brother Thomas Brooke, and their brother-in-law Daniel Buckley. In various combinations, the descendants of these men continued to operate the ironworks for more than eighty years.

*From the charcoal shed*

The furnace was repaired and improvements made. A stamping mill was constructed in 1805 to crush the slag and recover bits of iron. A small resmelting furnace was added to increase the output of castings. Between 1800 and 1824 the annual output of iron increased from 311 tons to 857 tons. The blast season was increased from less than 235 days to more than 300 days. The proportion of castings — stoves, pots, pans, kettles, mold boards for plows, machine parts, and other domestic, agricultural, and industrial items — increased and then surpassed the production of less valuable pig iron. With the completion of the Schuylkill Canal, Hopewell's heavy products could be shipped cheaply to Philadelphia and from there to markets as distant as Portsmouth, New Hampshire.

In 1828 the furnace at Hopewell was rebuilt, but ten years later it was outmoded: the hot-blast method of smelting with anthracite was introduced in 1838. Coal was far cheaper than charcoal, and labor costs for iron produced with anthracite were about 20 percent of labor costs for iron made with charcoal. The owners of Hopewell built an anthracite furnace in 1853, but it did not pay: the village was too distant from the coal fields. Production of cast objects ceased, but the village continued to make pig iron, for which there was an insatiable demand because railroads were expanding throughout the country. In 1853 Hopewell actually achieved its greatest output ever: 1,205 tons of pig iron. In 1858 it produced 1,094 tons. Thereafter, production declined. In a final effort to improve the competitiveness of their furnace, the owners in 1880 added a steam boiler to augment the water wheel, and in 1882 they installed a roaster to pretreat the ore. But the blast of 1883 was Hopewell's last.

For a period, mining and charcoal-making continued on Hopewell property in order to supply other furnaces. Quarrying rights were sold to a stone company. Fenceposts and rails were cut in the woods. The Big House was used as a summer residence, and the tenant houses were leased. So matters continued until 1935, when the National Park Service decided to restore the crumbling furnace. The U.S. government purchased about 6,000 acres surrounding the village, most of which later were transferred to the Commonwealth of Pennsylvania to create French Creek State Park. In 1938 Hopewell Village was declared a National Historic Site.

*PUBLIC TRANSIT:* None.

*AUTOMOBILE:* From Exit 23 off the Pennsylvania Turnpike, take Route 100 north toward Pottstown. After about 9 miles turn left onto Route 23 and continue 7 miles to an intersection with Route 345 on the right. Turn right and follow Route 345 north 4 miles to the entrance to Hopewell Village National Historic Site on the left.

*THE WALK:* From the visitor center proceed downhill to the charcoal hearth and shed, the ironmaster's house, the company office and store, the barn, the furnace and water wheel, and finally the tenant houses along the road south of the village.

Another point of interest is Lake Hopewell. From the charcoal hearth a wide trail leads west several hundred yards to the dam at the eastern end of the lake. From the southern end of the dam, another trail leads back to the village.

Near the entrance to Hopewell Village is the Baptism Creek Environmental Study Area, which includes a trail loop of ¾ mile. A brochure available at the visitor center provides directions and commentary.

# 18

# RIDLEY CREEK STATE PARK
## Northern Section

*Walking and ski touring — 5 miles (8 kilometers). A rolling landscape of former farms. The trail follows Ridley Creek upstream, then circles back through overgrown fields, woods, meadows, pines, and pastures. Within the park is the Colonial Pennsylvania Plantation, restored to resemble an eighteenth-century farm. Visitors can observe farm tasks performed with tools of the era. Ridley Creek State Park is open daily from 8:00 A.M. until sunset. Dogs must be leashed. Telephone for information about the horse livery. The park is managed by the Bureau of State Parks (566-4800). The Colonial Pennsylvania Plantation, which charges a small admission fee, is open April through November on Saturday and Sunday from 10:00 A.M. to 4:00 P.M., or until 5:00 P.M. when Daylight Savings Time is in effect. Dogs and picnicking are prohibited. Telephone for information regarding school or group tours. The plantation is managed by the Bishop's Mill Historical Institute (353-1777).*

---

**T**HE SMALL FAMILY FARM — America's quintessential agricultural unit — first flourished in southeastern Pennsylvania. From here spread the pattern that became the national norm: each isolated farmhouse surrounded by its own outbuildings, fields, and woodlot. Yet this form of rural development and agricultural organization is not at all what William Penn had in mind for his colony three hundred years ago.

Penn was a strong believer in community institutions and mutual aid. He thought that settlers should live in agricultural hamlets located at the center of small, tidy townships. "For the

more convenient bringing up of youth . . . so that neighbors may help one another . . . and that they may accustom their children also to do the same," Penn advocated the establishment of hundreds of villages where farmers, craftsmen, tradesmen, teachers, ministers — in fact, all rural residents — would live near a meetinghouse or church.

Penn published two township plans showing suggested farm shapes and sizes. According to both proposals, townships were to consist of 5,000 acres. The boundaries and road pattern would be rectilinear. One plan suggested up to twenty farms of 100 acres each, bordering a road that divided the township in half. The remaining land would be reserved for children of the original settlers. According to the other plan, ten houses would occupy lots of 50 acres each at the township center, from which ten wedge-shaped farms of 450 acres each would radiate outward to the edge of the township.

To some extent Penn's township plans reflected the typical European village of the feudal era, with its tradition of communal decision-making and cooperation. Indeed, as proprietor of Pennsylvania, Penn possessed many feudal powers. Under his charter he could and did demand perpetual quitrent from the settlers in lieu of feudal services. And his land grants provided for escheat — reversion of the land to him — if an area remained unoccupied three years after being granted to a settler.

At first the process of surveying and occupying the Pennsylvania countryside proceeded in an orderly fashion, but few of the many townships that were established conformed to the village pattern Penn advocated. Newtown near Ridley Creek State Park was one of the few townships that actually developed into a village, since the overwhelming majority of farmers preferred to build homes in the middle of their own fields. Community institutions, such as meetinghouses, schools, mills, inns, and stores, were scattered without thought to the township centers or to any particular plan. Even as late as the 1790s a traveler observed that between Philadelphia and Lancaster he found "not any two dwellings standing together," except at Downingtown.

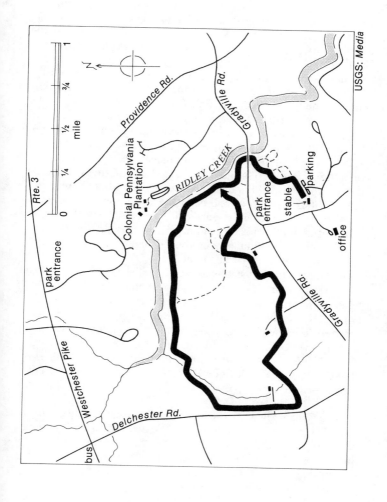

Several explanations have been offered to account for the development of dispersed, individual farms in America and the rejection of agricultural villages similar to what many settlers had known in Europe. With notable exceptions (such as the Moravians), the settlers did not like communalism: economic individualism was the prevailing philosophy. Farmers wanted to make their own decisions and to reap the full and exclusive benefit of their own efforts. As a matter of simple convenience, travel time to and from the fields was reduced by living at the center of the farm. Because relations with the Indians in eastern Pennsylvania were peaceful, settlers did not have to live in villages for mutual defense, which at first was thought necessary in New England. There the villages were surrounded by open fields and each farmer was granted several small, scattered parcels in order to guarantee an equitable distribution of different qualities of land, as had been done in Europe. But even in New England, settlers began to disperse to scattered family farms after 1680. The agricultural village was also on the wane in Europe, as communally cultivated fields were enclosed to create large privately owned tracts.

The family farm system was well established in Pennsylvania by 1700, but during the following century family holdings tended to shrink with each generation as lands were divided among sons, for the English custom of primogeniture was rejected in Pennsylvania. By 1760 the average farm in Chester County (which at that time included Delaware County) was about 125 acres. At least a dozen of these old farmsteads still stand in Ridley Creek State Park. A similar pattern of small, closely spaced farms is evident at Tyler State Park (see Chapter 10).

On a typical eighteenth-century farm, a wide variety of crops and livestock was raised for home use and for sale. Between a half and two-thirds of production was consumed on the farm. Still, most Pennsylvania farmers aimed for more than bare self-sufficiency, so that an international market economy developed, with particular emphasis on wheat.

James T. Lemon in *The Best Poor Man's Country*, a geographical study of early southeastern Pennsylvania, estimates that the typical farmer in 1760 planted yearly about 8 acres in wheat at a yield (very low by modern standards) of about 10 bushels per acre. About 2 acres were planted in rye, yielding 12½ bushels per acre. Both wheat and rye were sown in autumn and harvested in late spring or early summer. Other grains were planted in spring: about 4 acres of oats, 2 acres of barley, 2 acres of buckwheat, and 8 acres of Indian corn — all yielding 15 bushels per acre. Wheat brought the highest price, and substantial quantities of flour were sent to Philadelphia and Baltimore for export to the West Indies, southern Europe, and England. Wheat also was distilled for whiskey, as was rye. Oats were used primarily for horsefeed and barley for beer. Buckwheat was eaten by the poor or was plowed under to improve the soil. Corn primarily was fed to hogs and other livestock. Other crops grown in small quantities were potatoes, turnips, and flax for linen, linseed oil, and fodder. About 20 acres on a typical farm were planted in hay, which was mown twice yearly. Perhaps 25 acres were forest, a valuable crop in an era when wood was the only fuel. The remaining acreage was fallow.

Virtually every farm had an orchard. One writer in 1748 stated, "Every countryman, even the poorest peasant, had an orchard with apples, peaches, chestnuts, walnuts, cherries, quinces, and such fruits, and sometimes we saw vines climbing in them." Apples were grown for cider, and an orchard of fifty trees was considered small. The average farm had about 2 acres devoted to orchard, at sixty to seventy trees per acre.

Just as eighteenth-century farmers did not specialize in production of a single crop, so a variety of livestock was raised in modest numbers. The average farmer might have a half-dozen cattle, including three cows. In fact, Chester County gradually became known for its production of cheese. Three to four horses were common, since they were all-purpose draft animals. Eight to ten swine and as many sheep were also usual, the former for meat and the latter for wool. The amount of pork consumed was approximately twice that of beef. Chickens, ducks, geese, turkeys, and other fowl were raised for meat and eggs. Finally, one or two hives of bees were kept for honey and to pollinate the fruit trees and clover.

Field rotation was standard practice, but fertilizing was not. Because of the emphasis on wheat as the main cash crop, livestock herds were slim and so, in consequence, was manure. After 1750 lime and gypsum were introduced as fertilizers, but they were not popular, perhaps because those who experimented with these products applied too much and hurt their soil. More usual was a simple reliance on a three-field or four-field rotation pattern, with one field being left fallow each year or perhaps planted in clover. Sometimes exhausted fields were left fallow for many years and allowed to grow into scrubby woods.

By modern standards the typical eighteenth-century Pennsylvania farm was deficient in other ways also. Before 1750 barns were the exception rather than the rule: hay was left in stacks and livestock were wintered in the open, often simply in woodlots or fallow fields. The great barns of the Pennsylvania Dutch were not built until after the Revolution. Tools also were primitive. Light wooden plows with strips of iron on the moldboards could not penetrate deeply into the soil, so fields had to be plowed three times. Cast-iron plows were not introduced until the end of the eighteenth century. Harvesting also was laborious: grain was cut with hand sickles, and threshing was done with flails or by treading on the sheaves.

In general, then, the typical farm in southeastern Pennsylvania during the eighteenth century was a family operation producing a variety of food for home consumption, a small surplus of vegetables and livestock for market, and a large surplus of wheat. Agricultural reformers of the day lamented the lack of fertilizing and poor animal husbandry, but they failed to recognize that most farmers were comfortable and so saw little reason to change.

*PUBLIC TRANSIT:   From 69th Street Terminal, take SEPTA bus 104 west via West Chester Pike (Route 3). Ask the driver to let you off at the intersection with Delchester Road 4 miles west of Newtown Square. You will know that your*

*stop is coming after the bus passes Plumstock Road on the right. For the return trip, flag the bus as it approaches.*

*From the intersection of West Chester Pike and Delchester Road, walk 1 mile south on Delchester Road to a gravel drive intersecting from the left. Enter the drive but then immediately turn right onto a narrow path. Continue around the trail circuit described below.*

AUTOMOBILE: *From Newtown Square, which is located 8 miles west of Philadelphia on West Chester Pike (Route 3), go west on Route 3 a little more than 3 miles to the entrance to Ridley Creek State Park on the left. Turn into the park and follow the curving park road 2 miles to Gradyville Road, passing (at 1.3 miles) the parking lot for the Colonial Pennsylvania Plantation. At Gradyville Road, turn right and go 0.7 mile to another park entrance. Turn left and follow the park road 0.4 mile to a road leading left toward the stable and picnic areas 8 and 9. At the next intersection turn left again toward the stable and a large parking lot.*

THE WALK: *This walk follows a bridle path that at first passes through several horse pastures. If at any point you find the trail barred by a gate or rail fence, be sure to leave the gate or rails as you found them.*

*From the cylindrical turret at the corner of the stable, follow the bridle path uphill away from the building. Bear left on the horseshoe trail and continue straight downhill past a path intersecting from the right. Bear left at a four-way trail junction. Near the bottom of the slope, descend steeply between wooden posts to the edge of Ridley Creek. (The way is sometimes barred by rails between the posts.) Turn left under the Gradyville Road bridge. Follow a broad path that at first veers left away from the creek, then bends right to rejoin the river. Continue straight past a trail intersecting from the left. (You will return by this other trail later.)*

*Continue with the creek below to the right. Eventually curve left through a partial clearing. On the far side of the* creek is the Colonial Pennsylvania Plantation. Continue straight past a path intersecting from the left. Descend into the woods and past another trail leading left. Gradually the trail curves left, then right across a stream, and left again uphill. For a period the trail runs parallel with Delchester Road, at one point crossing a gravel drive. (If you came by bus, join the trail here.)

After crossing the gravel road, turn left at the next trail junction. Descend through an overgrown field. Continue through a short stretch of woods. Follow the path between an overgrown field on the left and a hedgerow on the right. Turn right to continue between the field and hedgerow. Enter the woods and descend left. Cross a gravel road and continue somewhat uphill across a field. Pass through a hedgerow and continue along the edge of another field. Turn left into a pine plantation. After emerging from the woods, follow the path left, then right through scrub and overgrown fields. Pass a house on the right. Turn right at the far edge of the scrubby field. Follow the path downhill through the woods, at first gently and then steeply along the side of a ravine. At a T-intersection near Ridley Creek, turn right to return to the stable. (If you came by bus, do not turn right to go to the stable; rather, bear left and continue as described in the previous paragraph.)

# 19

# RIDLEY CREEK STATE PARK
## Southern Section

*Walking and ski touring — 5 miles (8 kilometers). Country roads, now closed to motor vehicles, form a large loop passing through wooded ravines and overgrown fields. A short spur leads to Sycamore Mills, the remains of an industrial hamlet of the eighteenth and early nineteenth centuries. Spring and fall birding is excellent along Ridley Creek. The park is open daily from 8:00 A.M. until sunset. Dogs must be leashed. Telephone for information about bicycle rental and fishing. Managed by the Bureau of State Parks (566-4800).*

---

"**W**HEAT IS THE GRAND ARTICLE of the province. They sow immense quantities," proclaimed the anonymous author of *American Husbandry,* commenting in 1775 on Pennsylvania agriculture. The emphasis on wheat brought the development of numerous small, water-powered gristmills along the region's rivers. A map of southeastern Pennsylvania published in 1792 shows mills of one sort or another — including gristmills, sawmills, fulling mills, linseed oil mills, paper mills, and other such works — located about every 2 miles on permanent streams. In 1782 Chester County (which until 1789 included Delaware County) had 123 gristmills, of which Sycamore Mills, now in Ridley Creek State Park, was one.

When first built in 1718 by John and Jacob Edge, this gristmill was called Providence Mill because it was located in Upper Providence Township. The mill stood on the northeast side of Ridley Creek about 125 yards upstream from the present-day Chapel Hill Road bridge. Here grain from nearby farms was

*Mill office (later Union Library)*

ground, using different sets of millstones for wheat, rye, barley, buckwheat, and corn. Most grain in those days was ground locally (if it was ground at all), because more than half of what was grown was used on the farm rather than sent to market.

In 1748 a sawmill was erected next to the Providence gristmill. The sawmill — powered by water from the same race and perhaps even by the same water wheel that served the gristmill — was operated only when the gristmill was idle. Both structures were demolished by fire in 1901.

Although the gristmill and sawmill are gone, the former office, a slender, two-story structure, still stands a few dozen yards up the road from the site of the mills. This building was fireproof. It had cement floors and (originally) a metal roof. In 1818 the second story was converted to the Union Library, a proprietary or subscription library that by 1834 had more than eight hundred volumes. The arrangement did not last, however, for in 1862 the library was liquidated and its books were sold at a sheriff's sale. Now the building is a private residence.

Behind the former mill office and library is another private residence, at one time a blacksmith and wheelwright shop built in the middle of the eighteenth century. Like gristmills, blacksmith shops were numerous; they might be compared to present-day service stations. Blacksmiths served a local clientele because much of their work involved custom-made fittings. For a period the shop was owned by Amor Bishop, grandson of Thomas Bishop, Sr., who acquired Providence Mill in 1781. The mill complex then came to be called Bishop's Mill. In 1868 ownership of the property changed again, and the mill was renamed Sycamore Mills.

Across the street from the site of the gristmill and sawmill is a large stucco house, which was the mill owner's residence. The oldest part of the house was built of logs early in the eighteenth century.

Next to the gristmill and sawmill but closer to the bridge over Ridley Creek a large, one-story rolling and slitting mill operated between 1810 and 1830. Iron hardware was fashioned from pig iron transported here from rural iron furnaces similar to Hope-

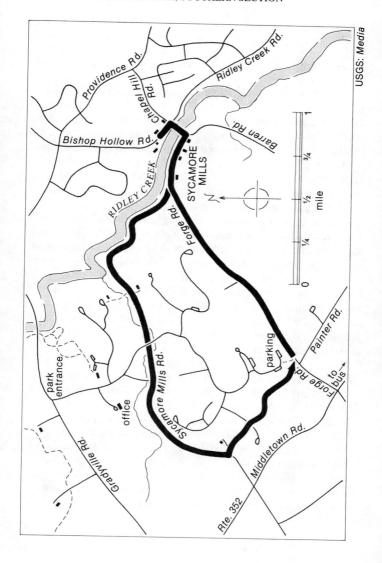

USGS: *Media*

well Furnace (see Chapter 17). The rolling mill eventually failed, however, probably because transportation costs were high compared to those of similar plants located near the new canals, improved turnpikes, and growing cities of the nineteenth century.

An old wagon shed still stands at the intersection of Bishop Hollow and Chapel Hill roads. The shed is thought to have been used in connection with the sawmill to shelter log-hauling equipment and, on the second floor, to store lumber. The walls of a barn built in 1848 and used to store grain are visible 40 yards up Chapel Hill Road on the left. The decrepit remains of a springhouse, where perishable food was kept cool during summer, are located in the woods next to Ridley Creek Road about 50 yards downstream from the bridge.

On the southwest side of Ridley Creek a small nail factory was located by the dam upstream from the bridge. Four houses stand at intervals along Sycamore Mills Road, with a small community bakehouse near the end of the bridge. Built between 1785 and 1830, the cottages were workers' homes during the hamlet's most prosperous period. But the failure of the rolling mill precipitated the community's gradual descent into the obscurity shared by the hundreds of other gristmills and small industrial operations that once were scattered throughout southeastern Pennsylvania.

*PUBLIC TRANSIT: From 69th Street Terminal take the Media Rail Line (SEPTA 101) to Bowling Green station in Media. From there catch SEPTA bus 77 for Granite Run Mall and Chester. Get off at the Delaware County campus of Pennsylvania State University. From the campus entrance walk north ½ mile on Middletown Road (Route 352) to an intersection with Forge Road. Turn right onto Forge Road and go ¼ mile to a barrier in the road just beyond an intersection with Painter Road. Pass the barrier and continue straight into the park on Forge Road.*

*Mill dam*

*AUTOMOBILE: From Newtown Square, which is located 8 miles west of Philadelphia on West Chester Pike (Route 3), follow Newtown Road (Route 252) south 1 mile. Turn right onto Gradyville Road and go 3 miles to the entrance of Ridley Creek State Park. Turn left into the park and follow the curving park road, continuing straight at each intersection. After passing roads for picnic areas 10 and 11-12-13, turn right and then right again for picnic area 15, which has two parking lots, one after the other.*

*Begin your walk on the gravel path where the park road curves left from the first parking lot to the second. Follow the gravel path 150 yards to join Forge Road near a barrier at the intersection with Painter Road. On the right note the bicycle path by which you will return at the end of your walk.*

*THE WALK: Although the roads followed by this walk are closed to most automobile traffic, be alert for bicycles and occasional park vehicles.*

*From the barricade at the intersection of Forge Road and Painter Road, follow Forge Road east for more than 1 mile to Sycamore Mills Road and Ridley Creek. To see the remains of Sycamore Mills, follow Sycamore Mills Road to the right (downstream), then return by the way you came.*

*From the intersection of Sycamore Mills Road and Forge Road, follow Sycamore Mills Road northwest with Ridley Creek on the right. Continue for more than 2 miles as the road curves left away from the river, passes some houses, and enters the woods. Continue through a short tunnel and past a road and bridge on the right.*

This bridge was part of the entrance drive for the Jeffords Mansion, which is now the park office. In 1966 Pennsylvania bought the 2,000-acre Jeffords estate for $5.6 million. An additional 500 acres was purchased from adjoining owners. Funds were provided by Project 70, a $70-million state bond issue voted for the acquisition of parkland.

Eventually, after Sycamore Mills Road climbs and curves left, it reaches an intersection with an asphalt bicycle path on the left. The intersection is further marked by the beginning of rows of trees along both sides of the road. Turn left onto the bicycle path, and follow it uphill and across an asphalt road. Continue to your starting point on Forge Road near the intersection with Painter Road.

# 20

# TYLER ARBORETUM

*Walking and ski touring — 3.5 miles (5.6 kilometers). Exotic trees, flowering shrubs, meadows, and woods — all interconnected by an extensive trail network. The arboretum is rich also in field and forest wildflowers. Open daily from 8:00 A.M. until sunset. Dogs must be leashed. Picnicking is prohibited. The house and library are open Sunday from 2:00 P.M. to 5:00 P.M., April through October. The house (decorated for the holidays) is also open during the week after Christmas. Managed by the John J. Tyler Arboretum (566-5431).*

---

THE LAND AT TYLER ARBORETUM first became a showcase for exotic trees during the middle of the nineteenth century. At that time the property was owned by the brothers Minshall and Jacob Painter, descendants of Thomas Minshall, to whom William Penn had granted the tract in 1681. The Painter brothers were prosperous Quaker farmers who read widely in the field of natural science. They inherited about 500 acres and added another 150 acres during their lives. They improved the property with springhouses, smokehouses, and other structures, including a library building. Between 1830 and 1875 they planted more than a thousand trees and shrubs, including many unusual species, on the slope below their house and barn. Some of these specimens survive, including a Cedar-of-Lebanon, a Common Baldcypress, and a Giant Sequoia. The Tyler Arboretum was established in 1945 by the bequest of Laura Tyler in honor of her deceased husband (and cousin), John J. Tyler. Laura Tyler was a great- (to the fifth power) granddaughter of

*Butterfly weed*, Asclepias tuberosa

Thomas Minshall. Her husband was a nephew of the Painter brothers.

Although Tyler Arboretum has large plantings of pines, hollies, magnolias, dogwoods, cherries, crabapples, rhododendrons, azaleas, lilacs, and other ornamental trees and shrubs, most of the land is meadow and woods. In contrast to the many varieties of cultivated trees and shrubs, the woods demonstrate that in a natural setting relatively few species predominate.

The climax plant community of southeastern Pennsylvania is the so-called "oak-chestnut" forest— somewhat of a misnomer ever since the early twentieth century, when chestnut blight killed all mature American Chestnut trees. The disease continues to kill chestnut saplings as they sprout from old root systems. North of the Potomac River, Tulip-trees (also called Yellow-poplar) have filled the gap left by the chestnuts and now occupy a position of co-dominance with the oaks. Beech, Black Cherry, and varieties of ash, hickory, and maple also are common. Dogwood is widespread in the understory.

Although many trees are tolerant of a broad range of soil and moisture conditions, some prefer a particular type of terrain where they flourish and even supplant other species. For example, Swamp White Oak generally grows in moist or even soggy soils, as its name suggests. Willow Oak and Pin Oak often are found in heavy bottomland soils. Most oaks, however, including White, Scarlet, Black, and Chinquapin Oak, prefer drier soils. Southern Red Oak usually grows in upland regions. Blackjack Oak, Post Oak, and to a lesser extent Chestnut Oak have a high tolerance for dry, gravelly hilltops or poor, sandy soils. So do the evergreen Eastern Red Cedar, Pitch Pine, and Virginia Pine, which are among the first trees to grow in abandoned fields. White Pine is another sun-loving tree found in former farmland, and often forms pure stands in sandy loam soils.

Each type of terrain is associated with certain groups of trees. Stream banks and bottomland support River Birch, Boxelder, Red and Silver Maple, Sycamore, Black Locust, American Elm, Sour-gum, Witch-hazel, and Black, Green, and Pumpkin

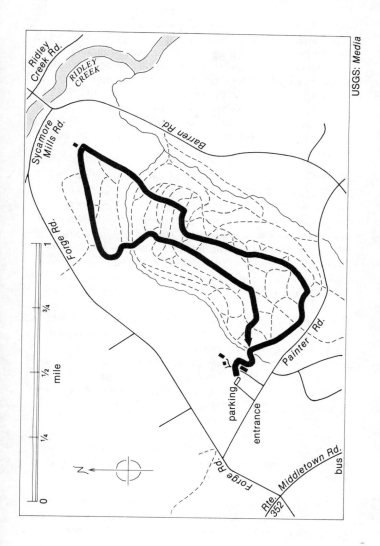

Ash. The slopes of hills and valleys sustain White Ash, Beech, Devil's-walkingstick, Mountain Maple, Striped Maple, Sweetgum, Tulip-tree, Flowering Dogwood, and Mountain Laurel. Cool, shady ravines and moist, north-facing slopes provide a suitable environment for Eastern Hemlock. On upper slopes and ridgetops the balance shifts toward the dry oaks and Shagbark and Pignut Hickory. As you follow the trails up and down the hills and stream valleys described in this book, and as the slopes face sometimes north and sometimes south, notice how the vegetation changes.

*PUBLIC TRANSIT:   From 69th Street Terminal take the Media Rail Line (SEPTA 101) to Bowling Green station in Media. From there catch SEPTA bus 77 for Granite Run Mall and Chester. Get off at the Delaware County campus of Pennsylvania State University. From the campus entrance walk north ½ mile on Middletown Road (Route 352) to an intersection with Forge Road. Turn right onto Forge Road and go ¼ mile to Painter Road. Turn right again and go another ¼ mile to the Tyler Arboretum entrance on the left.*

*AUTOMOBILE:   From Philadelphia follow City Avenue (Route 1) west past Media. Immediately after the divided highway ends (where the Media Bypass merges with Old Baltimore Pike), turn right onto Route 352. Follow Route 352 north 2 miles to an intersection with Forge Road. Turn right onto Forge Road and go 0.2 mile to Painter Road. Turn right again and follow Painter Road 0.2 mile to the Tyler Arboretum entrance on the left.*

*    Alternatively, from Newtown Square on West Chester Pike (Route 3), take Route 252 south to Route 1. Turn west on Route 1 and continue as described in the preceding paragraph.*

*THE WALK:   From the arboretum parking lot follow a path downhill past the end of a barn. Turn right onto a gravel road that leads along the lower side of the barn, where the ar-*

boretum education center and bookstore are located. Pamphlets summarizing the many programs and excursions sponsored by the arboretum are available.

Follow the gravel road as it curves left downhill. After crossing a small stream, fork right onto the Painter Brothers Trail. The route described below follows this trail for its entire length. The trail is blazed with red markers, but they are sometimes few and far between.

Follow the grassy track more or less straight, keeping Painter Road on the right. Veer left along the edge of the meadow where Dismal Run Trail (orange blazes) plunges downhill into the woods. Continue along the edge of a weedy field, through a short stretch of woods, and again along the edge of the meadow. Eventually, at a corner of the field, follow the path downhill into the woods.

Continue straight where several trails intersect. Gradually curve right, then turn abruptly left to follow the red-blazed path. Pass through a series of trail junctions as the path descends steeply. At the bottom of the slope, cross a stream and continuè straight through the woods.

At an abandoned stone house, turn abruptly left. Follow a dirt road through the woods, past a clearing, gradually uphill, then down and around to the left. Turn right across a stream on a wide path marked with red and white blazes. Pass through a crossroads and climb half-left. Continue past diverging trails as the main path curves uphill to the right. Pass through another crossroads. Continue along the left edge of a dogwood grove, then straight across the meadow on a faint track. Fork right to follow the red blazes through an area of rhododendrons. Turn left, then right to return to the barn and parking lot.

# BIBLIOGRAPHY

*Numbers in parentheses at the end of the citations refer to the chapters in this book that are based on the cited material.*

Adams, Alexander B. *John James Audubon*. New York: G. P. Putnam's Sons, 1966. (15)

Ballard, Francis and Marion Rivinus. *Guide to the Wissahickon Valley*. Philadelphia: Friends of the Wissahickon, Inc., 1965. (4)

Borror, Donald J. *Common Bird Songs*. New York: Dover Publications, Inc., 1967. (14)

Brady, Alan, W. Ronald Logan, John C. Miller, George B. Reynard, and Robert H. Sehl. *A Field List of the Birds of the Delaware Valley Region*. Philadelphia: Delaware Valley Ornithological Club, 1972. (1, 14)

Brandt, Francis Burke. *The Wissahickon Valley*. Philadelphia: Corn Exchange National Bank, 1927. (4)

Brockman, C. Frank. *Trees of North America*. New York: Golden Press, 1968. (7, 20)

Cantwell, Robert. *Alexander Wilson, Naturalist and Pioneer*. Philadelphia: J. B. Lippincott Company, 1961. (9)

Casey, William J. *Where and How the War was Fought*. New York: William Morrow & Company, Inc., 1976. (12)

Choate, Ernest A. *The Dictionary of American Bird Names*. Boston: Gambit, 1973. (9)

"City and Gulf Agree on Refuge Transfer." *The Beacon*, Philadelphia Conservationists, Inc., June 1955. (1)

Durant, Mary and Michael Harwood. *On the Road With John James Audubon*. New York: Dodd, Mead & Company, 1980. (15)

Fleming, Thomas. *1776: Year of Illusions*. New York: W. W. Norton & Company, Inc., 1975. (12)

Ford, Alice. *Audubon, by Himself*. Garden City: Natural History Press, 1969. (15)

Garrels, Robert M. *A Textbook of Geology*. New York: Harper & Brothers, 1951. (5, 10)

Goodwin, Bruce K. *Guidebook to the Geology of the Philadelphia Area*. Harrisburg: Pennsylvania Geological Survey, 1964. (5)

Grant, Robert R., Jr., and Ruth Patrick. "Tinicum Marsh as a Water Purifier," in *Two Studies of Tinicum Marsh*, The Conservation Foundation, 1970. (1)

Gruson, Edward S. *Words for Birds*. New York: Quadrangle Books, 1972 (9)

Hagner, Charles V. *Early History of the Falls of Schuylkill, Manayunk, Schuylkill and Lehigh Navigation Companies, Fairmount Waterworks, Etc.* Philadelphia: Claxton, Remsen, and Haffelfinger, 1869. (4)

Harding, John J. and Justin J. Harding. *Birding the Delaware Valley Region*. Philadelphia: Temple University Press, 1980. (1)

Hines, Bob. *Ducks at a Distance*. Ottawa: Canadian Wildlife Service, 1965. (14)

Hutton, Ann Hawkes. *George Washington Crossed Here*. Radnor, Pa.: Chilton Book Company, 1966. (12)

Kelley, Joseph J., Jr. *Life and Times in Colonial Philadelphia*. Harrisburg: Stackpole Books, 1973. (1)

Kemper, Jackson, III. *American Charcoal Making*. Eastern National Park & Monument Association. (17)

Klein, Esther M. *Fairmount Park, A History and a Guidebook*. Bryn Mawr, Pa.: Harcum Junior College Press, 1974. (2, 4)

Kurjack, Dennis C. *Hopewell Village*. Washington, D.C.: National Park Service Historical Handbook Series No. 8, 1954. (17)

Lemon, James T. *The Best Poor Man's Country*. New York: W. W. Norton & Company, 1976. (18, 19)

Marion, John Francis. *Famous and Curious Cemeteries*. New York: Crown Publishers, Inc. 1977. (3)

Martin, Joseph Plumb. *Private Yankee Doodle*. Acorn Press, 1979. (6, 16)

McCormick, Jack. "The Natural Features of Tinicum Marsh, with Particular Emphasis on the Vegetation," in *Two Studies of Tinicum Marsh,* The Conservation Foundation, 1970. (1)

McGinley, Anthony J. "A Thumbnail Sketch of Sycamore Mills." Pennsylvania Bureau of State Parks, 1978. (19)

McNeill, John T. *Rambling Along the Pennypack*. Philadelphia: Reliable Reproduction Co., 1963. (8, 9)

Morison, Samuel Eliot. *The Oxford History of the American People*. New York: Oxford University Press, 1965. (12, 16)

"Mount Auburn Cemetery," *Magazine of Cambridge,* Vol. 14, No. 7, April 1954. (3)

Pasquier, Roger F. *Watching Birds*. Boston: Houghton Mifflin Company, 1980. (14)

Peterson, Roger Tory. *A Field Guide to the Birds of Eastern and Central North America*. Boston: Houghton Mifflin Company, 1980. (14)

Peterson, Roger Tory. *How to Know the Birds*. New York: Mentor Books, 1949. (14)

Petrides, George A. *A Field Guide to Trees and Shrubs*. Boston: Houghton Mifflin Company, 1958. (7, 20)

Platt, Rutherford. *American Trees, A Book of Discovery*. New York: Dodd, Mead, & Company, 1952. (7)

Prelini, Charles. *Dredges and Dredging*. New York: D. Van Nostrand Company, 1912. (1)

Rivinus, Marion W. *Lights Along the Schuylkill*. Chestnut Hill, 1967. (2)

Rivinus, Willis M. *A Wayfarers Guide to the Delaware Canal*. 1964. (13)

Robbins, Chandler S., Bertel Bruun, and Herbert S. Zim. *Birds of North America*. New York: Golden Press, 1966. (14)

Rush, F. Eugene. *Geology and Ground-water Resources of Burlington County, New Jersey*. State of New Jersey, Department of Conservation and Economic Development, Special Report No. 26, 1968. (11)

Rush, F. Eugene. *Records of Wells and Ground-water Quality in Burlington County, New Jersey*. State of New Jersey, Department of Conservation and Economic Development, Water Resources Circular No. 7, 1962. (11)

Smedley, Samuel L. *Atlas of the City of Philadelphia*. Philadelphia: J. B. Lippincott & Co., 1862. (2, 4, 8)

Stoudt, John Joseph. *Ordeal at Valley Forge*. Philadelphia: University of Pennsylvania Press, 1963. (6, 16)

"Tinicum — A Chronology." *The Beacon,* Philadelphia Conservationists, Inc., March, 1978. (1)

"Tinicum Marsh Wildlife Area Saved — Future in Our Hands." *The Beacon,* Philadelphia Conservationists, Inc., June 1954. (1)

*Tinicum National Environmental Center: Master Plan*. U.S. Department of the Interior, Fish and Wildlife Service, 1980. (1)

*The Tinicum National Environmental Center, Master Planning and Environmental Assessment, Technical Memorandum I, Site Inventory and Analysis.* U.S. Department of the Interior, Fish and Wildlife Service, 1978. (1)

"Tinicum Wildlife Refuge Dedicated," *The Beacon,* Philadelphia Conservationists, Inc., January 1956. (1)

Trussell, John B. B., Jr. *Birthplace of an Army.* Harrisburg: Pennsylvania Historical and Museum Commission, 1976. (6, 16)

Trussell, John B. B., Jr. *Epic on the Schuylkill.* Harrisburg: Pennsylvania Historical and Museum Commission, 1974. (16)

*Visitor's Guide to the Centennial Exhibition and Philadelphia.* Philadelphia: J. B. Lippincott & Co., 1876. (2)

Walker, Joseph E. *Hopewell Village.* Philadelphia: University of Pennsylvania Press, 1966. (17)

Weygandt, Cornelius. *The Wissahickon Hills.* Philadelphia: University of Pennsylvania Press, 1930. (4)

White, Theo B. *Fairmount, Philadelphia's Park.* Philadelphia: The Art Alliance Press, 1975. (2, 4)

*Wissahickon Valley: Roads and Paths* (map with commentary). Friends of the Wissahickon, Inc., 1974. (4)

Yoder, C. P. "Bill," *Delaware Canal Journal.* Bethlehem, Pa.: Canal Press Incorporated, 1972. (12, 13)

# ABOUT THE AMC

The Appalachian Mountain Club is a non-profit volunteer organization of over 30,000 members. Centered in the northeastern United States with headquarters in Boston, its membership is worldwide. The AMC was founded in 1876, making it the oldest and largest organization of its kind in America. Its existence has been committed to conserving, developing, and managing dispersed outdoor recreational opportunities for the public in the Northeast. Its efforts in the past have endowed it with a significant public trust and its volunteers and staff today maintain that tradition.

Twelve regional chapters from Maine to Pennsylvania, some sixty committees, and hundreds of volunteers supported by a dedicated professional staff join in administering the Club's wide-ranging programs. Besides volunteer organized and led expeditions, these include research, backcountry management, trail and shelter construction and maintenance, conservation, and outdoor education. The Club operates a unique system of eight alpine huts in the White Mountains, a base camp and public information center at Pinkham Notch, New Hampshire, a public service facility in the Catskill Mountains of New York, five full service camps, four self-service camps, and nine campgrounds, all open to the public. Its Boston headquarters houses not only a public information center but also the largest mountaineering library and research facility in the U. S. The Club also conducts leadership workshops, mountain search and rescue, and a youth opportunity program for disadvantaged urban young people. The AMC publishes guidebooks, maps, and America's oldest mountaineering journal, *Appalachia*.

*We invite you to join and share in the benefits of membership.* Membership brings a subscription to the monthly bulletin *Appalachia;* discounts on publications and at the huts and camps managed by the Club; notices of trips and programs; and, association with chapters and their meetings and activities. Most important, membership offers the opportunity to support and share in the major public service efforts of the Club.

Membership is open to the general public upon completion of an application form and payment of an initiation fee and annual dues. Information on membership as well as the names and addresses of the secretaries of local chapters may be obtained by writing to: The Appalachian Mountain Club, 5 Joy Street, Boston, Massachusetts 02108, or calling during business hours 617-523-0636.